To: Jason Luis
with best wishes

A
Baby Boomer's Guide
To
Their Second Sixties

Supply Friendships

Remove Happiness

Live your show

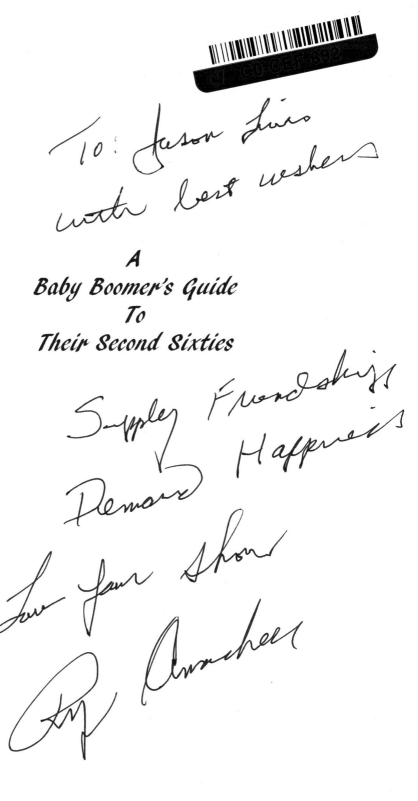

A
Baby Boomer's Guide
To
Their Second Sixties

Ryan Custer Amacher

SUNSTONE
PRESS

SANTA FE

Sunstone books may be purchased for educational, business, or sales promotional use.
For information please write: Special Markets Department, Sunstone Press,
P.O. Box 2321, Santa Fe, New Mexico 87504-2321.

Book and Cover design › Vicki Ahl
Body typeface › Minion Pro
Printed on acid-free paper
∞

Library of Congress Cataloging-in-Publication Data

Amacher, Ryan C.
  A baby boomer's guide to their second sixties / by Ryan Custer Amacher.
    p. cm.
  ISBN 978-0-86534-855-4 (softcover : alk. paper)
  1. Older people--United States. 2. Baby boom generation. 3. Aging. I. Title.
  HQ1064.U5A6445 2011
  305.260973--dc23
                    2011049948

WWW.SUNSTONEPRESS.COM
SUNSTONE PRESS / POST OFFICE BOX 2321 / SANTA FE, NM 87504-2321 /USA
(505) 988-4418 / ORDERS ONLY (800) 243-5644 / FAX (505) 988-1025

CONTENTS

11 Sports   172

12 Boomers and People Boomers Should Respect   186

13 The End: Not Death, the End of My Scouting Report   191

Source of Illustrations   196

Acknowledgements

Many friends, former friends and family pass through the pages of this book. It is startling to realize that some of the family is also in the former friends' category. Some may even be pissed to find themselves in it. I don't really care; I'm 65! Writing this book has been sobering in that you realize how fickle friendship really can be. But my father told me that! I thank them all, current and past. At one time or another they enriched my life. As I wrote this book I came to view my father as much smarter than I thought at the time. I wish I could tell him that.

The gang we met in Arizona when Susan was in real estate and I was an economist at Arizona State University plays a very significant role. They are fun and funny and they stay in touch, a trait I find attractive. Call a friend, current or past, today before it is too late. Remember, you are in your 60s.

First and foremost, I owe a great deal of thanks to my wife, Susan. Mostly I am grateful because after 46 years she is still here. She lived the pages of the book as much as I have. She lived most of it with me. I dedicate it to her. I could not have finished it without her help. I might not have lived it if she had not arrived at Ripon College in 1966.

When I first told her after prostate cancer that I was going to write a "story" about it, she did not laugh! Months later when I was working on an expanded manuscript, she did not complain. Instead she went to ride her horse, Thatcher (as in Margaret) and stayed away. Susan permeates the pages of this book. She is in essence the coauthor, silent coauthor. Most importantly she had to put up with my frank out bursts that piss family and friends off. She remains (mostly) amused. I should have anticipated this. She didn't flee in August 1966 when I met her at the Spot in Ripon the first week Ripon College had opened for freshman and transfer students. She introduced herself as Susan Mary Smith. I indelicately responded, "just an average girl?" The next night we met again at the water tower (another beer drinking venue). She slipped her date and met me back at her dorm. I think she initially mostly liked my Triumph Spitfire, but I won her over. The Spitfire comes to mind because it disappeared from the fraternity parking lot two weeks later and first year students were not allowed to have cars. Fifteen months later we were married.

Friends encouraged me with this project. Our friend and neighbor Gayle Momchilovich read and reread many versions of the manuscript. More importantly, she listened to repeated stories about this stuff. On top of everything, she and Don buy the type of gin I drink and they don't drink gin. We also agree on the smoking thing! We have great fun playing *Trivial Pursuit* in Don's garage/club house over drinks and an occasional "heater." We keep a running score and truth in advertising forces me to report that I am leading!

I met Patricia Tollison in August 1967, when I enrolled at UVA for graduate school. We are still friends. She came to my prostate cancer surgery and even learned how to clean the urine bag. That may define friendship. Patricia also read early versions of the manuscript and offered encouraging advice.

I went to high school with Mark and Jude Seidl. I had not seen them for more than 40 years, since their wedding! We reconnected by luck at a Badger/Gopher game in MSP. We have become good friends again. Mark did the cartoons for this book. I urge you to contact your old friends. It is prospecting, but there are some worthwhile nuggets out there.

Tom Hall, David Gray, and Ronnie Liggett read earlier versions and gave thoughtful comments. Barb Sellers gave helpful comments at a very early stage. I asked her if it was "too raw." Her response was, "you must not have read many books lately." Ginny Marzonni caught some errors, noted with a myriad of little yellow tabs. Grey Pierson read an early version and suggested the "Joy of Kegeling" concept. Jack Hickerson, a new friend, and retired college writing professor, gave early advice about diction that I did not understand. He is not responsible for anything!

Shawn Smith of Thomas Reprographics in Ft. Worth did his best fixing up the old pictures, one from 1953. He also took my author picture.

Finally, James Clois Smith, Carl, and the folks at Sunstone Press were helpful and encouraging. I hope they get rich.

Preface

Think how lucky we Boomers are. Our entire life span is the Golden Age of all American generations. It seems to me that it has all been about being in the right place at the right time. But there are issues you are going to experience as you age that are not "golden." They are not going to ruin your life, they are just going to change it. My wife's MD calls these changes "a series of glitches." These glitches will also change your golf game. Even Arnold Palmer looks like an old fart when he tees off at the Masters. This is an easy one to solve. If you are invited to be the honorary starter at the Masters, decline the invitation. The guys in your foursome don't care how you look when you tee off—they are aging right along with you.

We probably change more in a physical sense in the decade of our 60s than in any since our first decade. You need a guide to help as most of us are so spoiled we want things to be like we always expected them to be. They are appearing at an inconvenient time, our 60s, way too soon. "Those were the times, my friend, we thought they would never end." They do.

You need a guide to help you navigate your 60s. I will be your scout. Who we are and how we approach life is shaped by our history. I will review the important events in our Boomer experience and guide you through your new adventure. That adventure is the first half of your 60s. I will show the way. The journey is not something to fear. It should be approached with the same gusto we Boomers displayed in the 1960s. This "scouting" report will aid you in helping your parents in their old age, maneuvering through the maze of aging health issues; simple ones like cataracts and skin cancer. And scary ones like prostate cancer. If you approach these issues with the same sense of fun we Boomers have always had, you will be very loveable at 64.

It is not only the health issues, which we as Boomer men don't talk about, but relationship issues. Friends come and go. My father told me this, but I did not believe him about that either.

Some Boomers have children from third marriages making them uncles to your daughter's 20 year old college student from her second marriage. I think it has become so complicated that family reunions are falling by the wayside. In fact, they are declining in popularity. It is just too complicated and as we age it is harder to keep track of who we aren't talking to anymore.

The health issues seem front and center, but there all kinds of other issues. Our parents are dying and even if we don't want to be part of it, we are. I can give you some tips. Then there are a vast array of social issues we must deal with. They range from global warming, to race issues, to media, economics, and political issues. Then retirement. I don't know about you, but the real estate investments I planned on retiring on are now underwater.

This book is a practical guide to aging baby Boomers, to help you see the humor and irony in our wonderful Boomer ride. It will not make you younger, but I hope it can help you navigate some stormy seas.

1

Boomer Luck

We were born beginning on January 1, 1946. WWII had just ended. The war had put an end to the massive male unemployment of the Great Depression. Today young people find it hard to believe that in the 1930s few women worked outside the home. That point hit home for me when young people who read parts of an early version of this manuscript all questioned why the war put an end to male unemployment. The deficit spending on military stuff that would be blown up and replaced, and replaced again and again ended unemployment. The FDR acronym programs prior to WWII did not end the Great Depression; WWII did. The war caused a transfer of male workers into the military. They were replaced by females who were recruited into civilian war production putting almost all able bodied people to work. This was the seed of the women's movement. Rosie the Riveter probably had more impact on equal workplace rights for women than Gloria Steinem could ever have dreamed of. War production is, however, unproductive in a standard of living sense. The repressed citizens of the Soviet Union understood that they were first in space, first in vodka, but last in food. Civilians don't drive tanks and eat C-rations. Many commodities were rationed at home in the US to support the war effort. The standard of living did not improve until after the war ended. In this consumption sense, the Great Depression did not end until the end of WWII. Ironically, FDR did not play as big a role in ending the Great Depression and opening the door to our Golden Age as General Eisenhower did. But kids are not taught this in school. FDR gets the credit. This is probably taught to teachers in teacher reeducation schools. George Will once said, "Today there are more Marxists on the Harvard faculty than there are in Eastern Europe." I don't know if this is literally true, but I do know that if you remove the Engineering and Business faculty, the remaining faculty are mostly pink. And I don't mean skin color, but that would be also true.

We, the Boomers, were created by post-WWII America. This was the beginning of our great ride. It created our personal golden chariot. The first great transformation came right when we were being born. Our timing was magnificent. Maybe we should say our parents' timing or for many of us, their lack of planning, was fortunate for us.

I was born on November 9, 1945. That makes me 52 days too old to be officially a member of the Baby Boom generation, which is dated from January 1, 1946, to December 31, 1964. The peak year for births in the Boomer Generation was 1957. During this whole Boomer period, 76 million babies were born in the US.

I missed the Boomer generation by 52 days, but I am in no way a member of the Generation called the Silent Generation, those born between 1925 and 1945. This group was 16 years old when WWII started and most of them that were healthy ended up in the war. Tom Brokaw labeled those that grew up in the Great Depression and went on to fight in WWII, "The Greatest Generation." That group included the men and women who fought abroad and worked at home to defeat the Germans and the Japanese. Until Brokaw coined the term it had not been used to describe a demographic group. It has now replaced the official categorization.

The "official" names for the US generations are:

1900–1924 G.I. Generation
1925–1945 Silent Generation now Greatest Generation
1946–1964 Baby Boom Generation
1965–1979 Generation X
1980–2000 Millennials or Generation Y
2000–Present New Silent Generation or Generation Z

I am so close to the Boomers that I am much more comfortable with them than even my slightly older acquaintances, so I claim to be a Baby Boomer. In this sense, I am like an Indian scout for the cavalry. I am comfortable with this scouting task as my middle name is Custer. Keep in mind that General George Armstrong Custer did not get himself and all his men killed by bad scouting. His Crow Indian Scouts warned him that there was a large encampment along the Little Bighorn River. Custer had 208 officers and men with him. Estimates of the Lakota, Sioux, and Cheyenne were as high as 5,000. What this underscores is the importance of listening to your scouts to make better informed decisions. Actually, most of us would have never heard of The Battle of Little Bighorn if it were not for the fact that Otto Becker created a chromolithograph in 1896 entitled, "The Custer Massacre at Little Bighorn June 25th 1876." The lithograph was commissioned by Anheuser Busch. It was made from a painting by Cassily Adams entitled "Custer's Last Fight" It was given to bars by Anheuser Busch and is reportedly still in some. That's more than 100 years of beer company sponsored bar art; what a great country we live in.

There is even generational irony in my naming. My parents' pediatrician was Dr. Custer. The story that was told to me was that after the birth of the twins, as Becky and I were always called, Dr. Custer gave my mother an injection of something that put her into a coma for over a month. During that period he gave close attention to her care. She recovered and instead of suing, they were so grateful that they named me after him, making my name Ryan Custer. In 1945, MDs did not get sued! When I was a kid I took a lot of kidding about my middle name. Think of it—I could have had a trust fund; instead I got a funny middle name. In the 1950s, my friends, of course, called me, "custard pie."

Like an Indian scout with the cavalry, I am not a member of the Boomer Tribe, but I have lived with them and I know their ways. I was born before it was called the Baby Boomer Generation. Indeed, there was not even a Boom yet. I can move about freely, often undetected. The only Baby Boomer skill I was unable to pick up was rhythm, so to conceal my identity I stay off the dance floor. I am your scout. I am an observer and commentator, an advance scout, learning the terrain and reporting back to you on what to expect.

As Baby Boomers we have witnessed a lot of change. Most of these changes have affected us in a very positive way. Those that didn't, we ignored. We have done what we wanted; let the world adjust to us. I am trying to figure out where that trait comes from—most likely from Dr. Spock's influence on our parents.

I chuckled while watching the last Republican National Convention in St. Paul. There was 72-year-old John McCain embracing the 17-year-old pregnant, unmarried daughter of his female running mate in front of 5,000 Republican delegates. Republican delegates. How times have changed in our lifetime.

In the early 1960s, when we were in high school, pregnant girls just disappeared. They were there one day and gone the next. This puzzled me. Where did they go? I guess city girls went to Milwaukee and farm girls stayed home. Farm girls got married and city girls gave the child up for adoption. Neither group returned. They dropped off the face of the earth. I still don't know where they are. Most don't come to class reunions. This is difficult to understand as Boomers are not judgmental about unplanned pregnancies.

Then we went to college and nobody got pregnant, unless they wanted to. And some wanted to. The birth control pill was invented and was widely available on campus. They even gave them away on many campuses. Some social conservatives thought this was subversive. I didn't understand this even then. If social conservatives thought giving the pill away was subversive, did they prefer abortions? Come to think of it, abortions then were mostly done with coat hangers in back rooms. At least that is what we were told. We have come a long way baby.

The inventor of the pill was Carl Djerassi. Ever heard of him? He was born in Vienna to Jewish parents. He escaped the Nazis by moving to Bulgaria in 1939 and to the US in 1941. He attended Kenyon College and got a PhD from the University of Wisconsin. We are very lucky he got away from the Nazis. Imagine all the great inventions we don't have from smart Jews who did not get away from Hitler. Think of the lost inventions that died in the Nazi death camps. That's a very real opportunity cost of that bastard, Hitler.

Years ago, I read a very entertaining novel about a fraternity at the University of California in the very early 1960s. The title is *Goat Brothers* (Larry Colton: Dell Publishers, 1994). It was written by a sports writer and had real world characters. They are so real world that you would recognize some of the names if you read it. I recommend it highly. In this book, it seems like every sorority girlfriend gets pregnant. I first thought these only slightly older brothers must have been unluckier than we were. But, that is not the reason. The reason was there were no birth control pills. Just four years later, no girlfriends got pregnant. Now there was a paradigm shift that was significant. The inventor of the pill had as great an economic impact on us as Jonas Salk and hardly anyone knows his name. I repeat, Carl Djerassi. It might be that we never learned his name as no one could pronounce it.

Skip ahead to the present. We have had another fertility paradigm shift. Connecticut teenagers actually signed a pact to get pregnant. Some even had sex with street bums to get pregnant. My God, am I getting old or what? Street bums; so much for the "sweet smell of romance."

Back to St. Paul and the Republican Convention we see Sarah Palin and her family being greeted by nominee John McCain. The group included Bristol Palin, the pregnant seventeen year old and her boyfriend, Levi Johnston.

Perhaps, even more significantly, was that I saw this picture on the front page of *The Wall Street Journal*. Now that is real change. "The Wall" as many dedicated readers refer to it, started printing pictures in 2008, even color pictures on the front page. The treatment of Bristol Palin struck me as a sexual metaphor for the Baby Boomer generation. From disappearance or marriage, to pill driven freedom, to sought pregnancy, to acceptance of an unmarried couple by the (female) VP candidate of the Republican Party. All on TV and the front pages of *The Wall Street Journal*. All this seems fine to me, but if Republicans are so flexible with this, why do they find it so hard to legalize pot? And how about Levi Johnston, didn't he turn out to be a loser? His behavior might be the one argument in favor of street bums. At least one would know what she's getting and have no expectations for the future.

The great changes that have taken place in our lifetime have been good for most of us. It has significantly increased our freedom and our ability to pursue our dreams. As we turn 64, many of the changes are not going to be such fun. I chuckled (to myself) last week as my wife asked me to hook her bra in the back. Her rotator cuff injury prevented her from completing this simple task. Now there is a Boomer change. As teenagers we practiced a deft finger movement to remove the clasp—now we do the reverse, we help put them on. Many of the changes are not this trivial and much less funny. As your scout, my intention is to alert you, advise you, and provide a map of the terrain; let's get started.

2

Our History, Our Present, Our Future

Until recently, I thought that our Boomer future would be difficult. We would face hostility because of the economic burden we would impose on younger folks. Think of it. In 2012, Boomers start turning 66. At 66 we qualify for full Social Security and will comprise 25% of the population. Our 25% of the population will become income transfer recipients from younger taxpayers for the rest of our lives, maybe as long as 30 years. In many cases, these transfers will be from taxpayers at lower levels of income and wealth. We will consume huge portions of tax receipts and will not contribute much to national income. The burden will be on younger income earning, taxpaying folks. Of course, this burden will depend on birth rates and legal immigration. Immigration is a very interesting topic on which we could spend much time. We are all the progeny of immigrants, except of course for Indians. They are the Native Americans.

Since all of us except these Native Americans have immigrant ancestors, it is surprising that we see so much antagonism toward immigrants. The American Indians don't seem to mind, but then they have casinos.

A few summers ago, a surprisingly large number of the affluent women from the Greatest Generation who live in Minnesota where I do, began sporting buttons that had American flags as the background and said, "SPEAK ENGLISH PLEASE." Now, this is in North Central Minnesota where the locals are mostly descendants of Swedes, Norwegians, and Germans; go a little north to the Iron Range one finds the group that came to mine ore. There are huge numbers in "The Range" from an array of Central and East European countries. Now, none of these immigrant ancestors, mostly great grandparents, spoke English. If they had been forced to speak the native language, we would still be speaking Ojibwa in Northern Minnesota.

Let's get back to our grandparents. Foreign newspapers (mostly German) flourished in Wisconsin until the start of WWII. In the part of North Central Wisconsin where I was born, the Lutheran Church's early service was in German—even after WWII. Even as late as the early 1960s when I left for college. There is one sense in which this immigration was different. First, it was a much more orderly immigration. There were not many reported cases of people sneaking in. Immigrants came by ship. Criminals and sick people were loaded on another ship and sent home. And most immigrants maintained their home language for talking to each other, but did not allow their kids to speak the native tongue. If you think about it, that was very efficient. Many had big families and worked hard and long days. The houses were crowded and mother and father could have private time at home in a crowd. I fondly remember my paternal grandparents doing this. My grandfather didn't speak very much, but when he said something to grandma in Switzerdeutsh, she often smiled.

Enough social commentary for now. Let's get back to my fears for our old age. Because of these huge forced transfers of Social Security payments and medical payments from poorer working stiffs to richer Boomers, I feared that we would be compelled to hide out in our retirement communities. The young would resent us because they would understand that we were consuming more than our "fair share" of income. It is estimated that 57% of Boomers will outlive their money and will not be able to meet "basic needs," whatever that means. The young will be forced to pay much higher taxes to transfer services to the growing number of Boomers who are richer than they are. I feared we would be forced to hide out in armed retirement ghettos because we would be viewed by working younger folks as predator/scavengers, like the wolves of the late 19th century. There would be a bounty on us. We would be shot on sight and our ears cut off and taken to the county courthouse to collect the bounty from the branch of county government that was charged with eradicating "nonproductive" citizens. Taxpayers would see the economic sense in reducing the size of these unproductive tax revenue sucking pigs; not wolves, Boomers.

I recently noticed in the AARP magazine that Albert Brooks (63) has written a book, soon to be a movie, that tells the real story of America in 2030. In his movie, "resentment gangs" shoot up busloads of "olds," hijack a retirement ship, and bomb the AARP HQ.

I now think this will not happen. I have changed my mind, calming my fears. At this point it appears that the younger generations have become too soft, too "socialized" for this to happen. I think Albert Brooks's idea is very funny, but it won't happen. The reason it won't happen is actually a product of social engineering in the schools. I don't know if it fits in the giving back or paying forward category. I guess it would be giving back if they realized how much older people have contributed to them, or it would be paying forward if they are doing it so they won't be killed when they are old. This would be a type of old age insurance. I'm sorry, it may be the economist in me, but I always look for self interest even in the paying forward and giving back category. Don't you think athletes who do this are doing all this back and forth giving to increase their own marketability and income? It's all so hard to keep straight. More on this later. Again, luck hits the Boomers. Let's spend a little time reviewing our lucky Boomer history.

The End of WWII: The Start of It All

On May 7, 1945, the Germans surrendered to General Eisenhower in Rheims, France, and to the Soviets in Berlin. President Truman named the next day, Victory in Europe, V—E Day. Later the same summer, on August 6, the Enola Gay dropped the atomic bomb on Hiroshima. On September 2, 1945, General MacArthur, the Supreme Commander of the Allied Powers, accepted the unconditional surrender of the Japanese aboard the USS Missouri in Tokyo Bay. This was a great day for America. Make no mistake about it; in the 40s, "Japs" were real bastards. They sneak attacked us in Pearl Harbor, plundered parts of China, forced large numbers of Asian women into prostitution, performed medical experiments on American prisoners of war, and flew suicide planes at our ships. Perhaps most disgusting, if there are degrees of disgusting, were the atrocities committed in the Rape of Nanking. In Nanking in 1938, the Japanese Army reportedly killed more than 350,000 non-combatants. Unimaginable rape and torture was Japanese policy in Nanking and everywhere else in the Pacific Theatre. The Japanese government still does not own up to its complicity. An owning up would be a good start. Recently, there was flap in the press about President Obama's not attending a Japanese memorial for those killed by US atomic bombs. I say nonsense. I remember the Japanese started the war. President Truman was told that a conventional attack on Japan would be very costly in American lives. The bomb saved many of these lives. Most German leaders acknowledge the Nazi death camps. I would say it is way past time for the Japanese leaders to acknowledge their own history. And, I have not even brought up the Bataan Death March. I took all this to mean that President Obama learned some Japanese history when he was a student in Hawaii.

The War was finally over. The troops started to come home in droves. In

1945, over 15 million GIs, mostly men, returned to the US. Many of them had been away from home for years. There were no tours of duty in WWII; troops stayed until the end of the war. These men, many from farm communities, learned about sex in the military even FRENCH sex, as in French kissing, French tickler, and French tricks. My father-in-law, who was much older when he was drafted, had been a hotel manager. Because of his hotel experience, he became General Maxwell Taylor's mess sergeant. He lived to be 95, and later in life was fond of telling stories to my wife, his daughter, when they were alone. Stories of young French women and champagne bottles lowered on pink ribbons into cold well water to chill. Oh, those village girls. I suspect that most vets have fewer of these fond memories. Most didn't have access to a General's wine supply.

The returning vets were ready to start making up for lost time. These troops, Tom Brokaw's inspiration for the Greatest Generation, wanted to make up for lost time. They went back to school in droves under the GI Bill. The returning vets, with government support, spawned the greatest increase in higher education that the US had ever seen. Before this time, mostly rich kids went to college. Public institutions were small and not viewed as highly as private schools. Public colleges and universities grew rapidly because of these vets. Many of these vets were married and the Land Grant colleges built housing for them. Some of this housing was still in use in the 1980s, when Boomers' children attended these same colleges.

The fathers of the first wave of Baby Boomers were prolific breeders, learners, and workers. Americans began to transition in earnest and with great energy from a war economy to a peace economy. That meant shifting from producing military goods to producing consumption goods and creating infrastructure, like Eisenhower's interstate highway system.

By definition, we Boomers have no direct memory of WWII. But for some of us, stories lingered and we remember them. This oral history was blunt. Folks were not yet politically correct. I have one very distinct memory of this period. It centers on the disgust that the folks felt toward "draft dodgers." It was real and lasting. In the area where I grew up, young men could get out of the military if they were a "needed" farmer or went to work on the Alaskan highway. I remember hearing in the late 1950s, who these guys were. They were belittled and castigated at every opportunity, particularly at the VFW and the Legion, while the Vets were drinking and pitching horse shoes. It was not pretty language. Even as kids we could figure it out.

In the early 1950s, we ran around the neighborhood "barely" dressed with the neighbor kids. We sang a ditty that went, "Whistle while you work, Hitler was jerk, Mussolini lost his peenie, now it doesn't squirt." I am told that there were different versions in different parts of the Mid-West. For years I wondered where this came from, and the magic of Google allowed me to track it down. Iona & Peter Opie's *The Lore and Language of Children* reports it as, "Whistle while you work, Hitler is a jerk, Mussolini is a weenie." I like ours better, it sounded so dirty to us that it was great fun.

Between 1948 and 1958, 13 million new homes were constructed. In fact, the word "suburbs" was coined to describe the phenomenon. This also marked the beginning of the decline of many central cities. This decline has accelerated in recent years, and it was represented by the comedy of the absurd at the 2009 Super Bowl. Eminem, the white rapper, rapped an ode to the once great city of Detroit. His explanation of decline was grounded in racism and other sins of capitalism. But Eminem surely didn't take economics. He completely missed the cause of the decline. Thieving politicians, endless regulations, union leaders, high taxes , and crime are killing Detroit and other cities. Until this is reversed, most big cities in America will continue to decline. Recently, Andreas Apostolopoulos paid a bit over half a million dollars for the Pontiac Silverdome, $583K to be exact. It cost the taxpayers $55.7 million in 1967. He bought the property sight unseen while on vacation in Greece. One unsuccessful bidder planned to turn it into a land fill. They should have imploded it. My guess is that by selling it to an "investor" it will cost taxpayers much more than 10 times the original $55.7 public "investment" to "help" Apostolopoulos find a use for it. *Bloomberg Business Week* (August 8, 2010) referred to Apostolopoulos as a "daredevil entrepreneur." I think it would be more correct to think of him as a "governmental revenue entrepreneur." As my grandmother used to say, "You mark my words." I don't remember her ever being wrong. I wonder how he is going to deal with the fact that Detroit has $8 billion in debt which is 20% of the total Detroit property value. City tax revenue has dropped 12% since residents have left in droves and Chrysler went bankrupt. I suppose being a "daredevil entrepreneur" means one who tries to figure out how to get the federal government to bail Detroit out. What else could it mean?

In domestic politics, Joe McCarthy rose to power. Historians, who are mostly liberal, tell us that McCarthyism was a blot on the liberalism of the era.

McCarthy was elected to the US Senate from Wisconsin in 1946. By 1950, he had a reputation mostly for being a drunk. And keep in mind that Wisconsin is a drinking state. He was mostly viewed as a drunk by "pointy headed liberals" outside Wisconsin. I vaguely remember most people in rural Wisconsin thinking he was correct. This was double for sure the case in Wisconsin watering holes and there were many of these establishments.

Almost by accident, he hit on a novel campaign tactic to rejuvenate his reelection bid. McCarthy claimed in a speech to a women's group in Wheeling, West Virginia, that communists had infiltrated top levels of American government. This was at a time when Americans watched what Stalin was doing in Russia with a great deal of concern. "Tail Gunner Joe" gave powerful speeches, holding a sheet of paper that he claimed had the names of 205 men in the State Department who were members of the Communist Party. Spies! The speech was a hit with the silent majority, before they were called the silent majority. He went so far as to accuse General George Marshall, who at the time was serving as Secretary of Defense, of making "common cause" with Stalin on the strategy of the war in Europe and "marching side by side with him thereafter" (US Senate Speech, June 14, 1951). His attacks gave life to his 1952 reelection campaign, motivating him to make more claims against the "Godless Commies." He was reelected to the Senate in 1952.

He continued to call people to testify before his Senate Committee. Many were eager to implicate others to save themselves. The results were Black Lists that ruined many careers in the entertainment industry, particularly in Hollywood.

McCarthy was discredited when he moved the focus of his attacks from the pointy-headed liberals in the State Department and Hollywood. He switched his attention to the Defense Department. Keep in mind that the military and civilians in the Defense Department were heroes of the recent big war. The Army-McCarthy hearings lasted for 36 days and McCarthy was center stage looking for "Commies" in the military. His crudeness turned the public against him. Edward R. Morrow, the famous WWII reporter (who smoked on camera) exposed McCarthy on his program *See It Now*, a forerunner of *60 Minutes*. Murrow played tapes of his excessive questioning of witnesses before his committee. This was a stunning new method. Murrow did not editorialize. He let McCarthy's over the top questioning do him in. Most of us Boomers have few direct memories of this history. The oldest of us was only nine years old.

Perhaps even more importantly, many of us did not yet have a "new-fangled" TV.

McCarthy did have some lasting impacts. First, his demise established the political power of TV. Not only was TV entertaining, it became a major political tool, and is even more so today. Second, McCarthyism came to mean over the top witch-hunts led by mad men. History was forever after made in the media. Hardly anyone noticed, and it was not widely reported, that after the fall of the USSR and the Berlin Wall coming down in 1989, there was more than a little evidence in the Soviet archives that there were Commies in the State Department and some Commies in Hollywood. No one seemed to care. After all, we were told Communism was dead and who in the world would defend McCarthy. Let sleeping toxic subjects lie. It seems, in retrospect, that the self-destructive McCarthy was guilty of overplaying a pretty good political hand. (See Arthur Herman, *Joseph McCarthy: Reexamining The Life and Legacy of America's Most Hated Senator*, The Free Press, 2000.)

The Glorious 1950s: What a Great Time to Be a Kid

In 1950, we were in another war—this time in Korea. The Cold War had become hot when 90,000 North Korean troops, armed and trained by the Soviet Commies, invaded the Republic of Korea. President Truman acted immediately, the same day authorizing the US Navy and Army to "assist" the South Korean Army. Truman was a man of fast action. Compare that with today when we agonize for months about whether we should commit more troops to some hell-hole of a country. I believe Truman would say either send enough men to do the job or get out. As my grandfather used to say, "either shit or get off the pot." My grandfather was plain spoken like Truman and most of us had only one toilet.

Two days after Truman acted the UN adopted a cease-fire resolution. Then, as now, the UN was a debating society that existed mostly to accommodate good jobs and stealing opportunities by 3rd world bureaucrats (see P.J.O'Rourke, *Parliament of Whores, Grove*, 1991). It would be great if we could get these thieves out of New York. They hate America, they are exempt from many laws, they clog up the City, and they don't pay taxes. They are a pox on a great, thanks to Rudy Giuliani, American city.

Most of us don't remember much about the Korean Conflict part of our history either. And why was it a conflict instead of a war? A few of our fathers and uncles were called back into the service to fight yet again. We had McCarthyism, communism in Mao's China, and then the Korean Commies. The Cold War was very hot. On June 27, 1953, Armistice was signed in Panmunjom. The Conflict ended at the 38th parallel, creating North Korea and South Korea.

Some of our Boomer brothers have served time in the Army in South Korea, but by the time they got there, the shooting was long over. In fact we still have troops in Korea. About the worst things that happened to them were loneliness and VD. But we should not forget that 54,000 of our fathers and uncles were killed in the fighting—another 100,000 were injured.

We Boomers were leading a sheltered life during this period. We were mostly oblivious to the personal cost of Korea. We were young and unaware, our life was heavenly. We could race around town on our bikes. There were no seat belts in cars; we actually stood in the back seat. I can't remember when warnings started to appear on every product some do gooder group is worried about. We never heard that any of us were kidnapped, killed, molested, or gone missing. Our parents never cautioned us about strangers. The term "lock down" did not appear in our vocabulary. The only thing we worried about at all was that some of the people who we knew were watching us would report back to our parents about our behavior. It was a given that they knew who we were and they also knew our parents and grandparents.

In 1946, Dr. Benjamin Spock published *The Common Sense of Baby and Child Care*. In this popular book, Spock told our parents that they should let us be individuals. He told them that they should not concentrate on discipline. In essence, he told them that they should lighten up, although I am sure he did not use the term "lighten up." Lighten up is definitely a Boomer word. He told them "to feed us, love us, And leave us alone." That quote is actually a question in *Trivial Pursuit* and I got it right! This opened the door for us to "find ourselves." God bless you Dr. Spock.

Growing up in the 1950s was a care free experience. I actually never heard of child abuse. I am sure some fathers made their sons work too hard. Working too hard was surely true for the farm kids. Some kids got hit, but I did not observe much of this. I find it hard to believe that even Catholic priests (except maybe in Ireland) were molesting young boys back then. Monsignor Rueter, who bought Dodge cars from my Lutheran father rather than the Catholic

Chevy dealer, seemed very nice. I gave him a ride to the church many times when his car was in the shop. He never "hit on me." I surely would remember that. I do remember that he was usually drunk. If priests and teachers were "bothering" young boys back then, they sure were good at keeping it quiet. My wife thinks "things" happened, but it was too much for decent folks to believe, so they weren't disclosed. Usually, I am the cynical one in the family.

Our parents never warned us not to talk to strangers. We could go to public restrooms on our own. We could even pee outside. I don't remember anyone having a peanut allergy or for that matter, any type of food allergy. My twin sister tried to convince Grandma Amacher that she was allergic to sauerkraut, but Grandma did not buy into the argument. Have you ever wondered where these food allergies come from? I have a theory that they come from overprotective parents who don't let their kids eat things like peanuts (or dirt) that they have decided are bad for them, or maybe even food that they don't like themselves. As a result, they don't develop the protections in their gut to deal with them when they grow up. I have never told anyone this theory, as I am not sure it would hold up to empirical testing. If you took it far enough, you could argue that if you let a six month old smoke, say Lucky Strikes, the kids would develop protections that would let them smoke as adults with no ill effects. Maybe it is a good thing my wife and I decided not to have kids.

When we Boomers finally got to mow the lawn we came to the conclusion that it was work, not fun. This was a real learning experience. We were eager to try, but we quickly learned that work was, well work. We mowed the lawn shirtless and in bare feet. No sun protection, no safety glasses, no safety shoes, nothing. Interestingly, we survived. I don't remember anyone ever being hurt mowing a lawn. Last year, I saw a young boy mowing the neighbor's yard and he was all "safetied" up. He didn't look like a kid enjoying his first job—he looked like a HAZMAT worker. He had steel-toed shoes, plastic eye covers and ear protection. Think how new the word HAZMAT is.

I don't ever remember using sun screen and I know I had no idea what UV numbers were. Come to think of it, I never heard of anyone getting hurt from the sun, at least lasting hurt. Okay, a little skin cancer in old age. Who cares, it's only a few spots. In fact, if you don't have your readers on, you don't even see them. Even as teenagers we worried little about sun safety. The sun screen my wife and her friends used was baby oil with iodine mixed in it. It created an orangey tan on their white Minnesota skin.

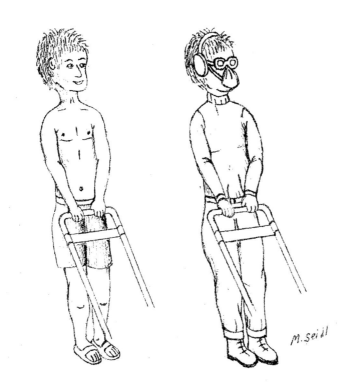

Mowing then – Mowing Now.

We spent many hours watching our feet through the x-ray machines at the Buster Brown Shoe Store. Did any of us get foot cancer? Not yet, anyway. We rode standing up in the car. In the winter, when we rode around with the windows up, our parents chained smoked. Our mothers drank and smoked when they were pregnant. They had not been "told" that their smoking would affect our brain power and who knows what else. Before my parents died, I told them that if they had been rich I would have sued them for limiting my potential. They thought the concept was amusing. For a very humorous account of growing up in Iowa in the same period, see *The Life and Times of the Thunderbolt Kid* (Bill Bryson, Broadway Books, 2006).

In North-Central Wisconsin, one of the great joys of winter was the toboggan chute, built by the CCC during the depression. A toboggan chute is sort of a roller coaster on ice, with the toboggan unconnected to the ice or the equipment. The geographic area of the chute was the same Chequamegon Forest where Edgar Sawtelle (*The Story of Edgar Sawtelle: A Novel*, Harper Collins, 2008) and his band of dogs were hiding out from the law, same time frame, different season. We rode it whenever we could get someone to take us. We didn't wear helmets. Helmets for activities did not even exist, except in football. The chute didn't have very high guides and no safety features. Parents didn't seem to care, and no one ever got hurt. I even heard stories of my father and his best friend, Jack Bauer, skiing on the chute. That made me think highly of my father. I suspect they must have been drinking beer before this activity, I am quite sure it was the only mind altering drug available at that time. The chute was closed in 1979 as insurance rates skyrocketed. It was too dangerous!

Unsafe Fun in the 50s.

I only remember our parents being afraid of two things. The most immediate fear was polio. In 1950, there were 150,000 cases of polio reported. Two years later the number of reported cases doubled to 300,000. Our relatives in the city sent their kids to live with relatives in the country, thinking it was safer. However, some little cousins were sent from the country to the city, the thought being it was safer there. The fear was made worse by the fact that nobody knew what caused it. My mother was sure it was swimming pools. We did not need to worry, because we didn't have swimming pools.

My parents noticed that I was limping and took me to see Dr. Meyer. After a spinal tap, he diagnosed me with polio. Soon after, yet another boy was diagnosed and we lived in the same apartment house. So much for mom's swimming pool theory. We were quarantined with a big red sign on the door. Walt Meyer, our Marcus Welby, came to visit every day. Teachers made daily house calls so I could keep up. Perhaps this was the start of home schooling. I owe these teachers. Now the teachers' union would probably prohibit them from this special treatment, unless of course they got special pay.

Three young boys in our area were infected by the polio virus. I was the luckiest. I came through with very few side effects. I have a slight weakness in a shoulder and a knee. I have always used it as an excuse for why I got the shit beat out of me in high school football. The second boy, the kid who lived in an upstairs apartment, still wears a shoe with a raised heel. Did you say infectious? The third, a good friend, was affected in his legs and he never walked again. This did not stop him from rough housing with us as we went through high school.

There was widespread fear of the polio threat. There were many pictures in the newspaper showing people in iron lungs, supposedly keeping them breathing. I still wonder what happened to them. I am sure there were some clips on the new fangled TV, which we did not yet have. The tower in Eau Claire did not broadcast as far as our little town.

Jonas Salk, the son of Russian-Jewish immigrants, went into high gear to solve this problem. A 1954 Gallop Poll reported that more people knew the full name of Jonas Salk than the full name of President Dwight David Eisenhower. Salk had to test his vaccine, so he, his wife, and three sons stepped forward. No one tried to take his kids away for endangering them. On April 12, 1955, the University of Michigan, where the testing was being monitored, announced that it was safe and effective. That was ten years to the day after the death of

Franklin Roosevelt, the most famous American polio victim. People around the nation celebrated the cure. So much for that scourge. It produced a great optimism that serious science and university research could solve real world problems.

The second thing our parents worried about were "Commies," again. These godless bastards stepped front and center, turning up the heat when they launched Sputnik 1 on October 4, 1957. It scared many Americans to their core, and for good reason. Lenin and Stalin had slaughtered millions of people and forced ruthless communism on the countries of Central and Eastern Europe. The "Cold War" seemed very scary.

Sputnik was Russian for "traveling companion." Many Americans translated this to mean "fellow traveler" a popular phrase of Joe McCarthy's in the Army-McCarthy Hearings. The heartland of America still believed that McCarthy was fundamentally correct and I remember that most all our parents knew it for sure when we listened to Sputnik's eerie beeping sounds on the radio. Less than a month later, Sputnik II was launched with the first fellow traveler aboard, a dog named Laika. The Commies did not provide for reentry so Laika became the first space casualty. US jokesters referred to Sputnik 2 as Muttnik. Sputnik 3 was a scientific laboratory launched in May, 1958. It degraded more rapidly than planned and in 1960 it burned up reentering the atmosphere.

Sputnik 4 was launched two years later and also burned up on reentry. Debris from the reentry was found in Manitowoc, Wisconsin, less than 100 miles from my home. Holy shit, we could be nuked from space!

President Eisenhower tried to reassure Americans that we didn't need to worry, but our parents sure did worry. We practiced duck and cover exercises in grade school instead of fire drills. We would duck under our desks to cover ourselves from the fallout from the nuclear bombs those Commie bastards would be dropping on us. Underground bomb shelters became popular and some were even built in our small, remote Wisconsin community. If people had thought about it rationally, they would have realized that there was no strategic interest in bombing a town in rural Wisconsin. A friend who grew up in Minneapolis remembers fearing bomb attacks, but it seemed irrational to me as all we had were cows and milk. But, our parents believed Commies were irrational. I suppose the present culture of "lock downs" is a similar genre, but it strikes me the kids today know these exercises are real and a threat, it likely frightens them. It is real because kids have guns and are crazy. I don't think any of us thought the Commie threat was real. We didn't think they were crazy. Most of us were amused. Way back then we understood mutually assured destruction. Mostly it meant we didn't have to do spelling. We were too busy doing duck and cover.

All this worry was, in retrospect, a blessing for us. We can thank the godless Commies for scaring politicians into action. We were about to enter high school and high schools were transformed for groups of students with high potential. It was okay to "pick" high potential students for special treatment and to discriminate on the basis of tests then. The University of Iowa was developing tests that measured "potential" and we all took them. It was important to be a good test taker then as opposed to the baloney we hear now. Baloney like, "my daughter is a great student; she just isn't a good test taker." I call a big BS on rationalizations about test taking. It ranks high on my parental BS Geiger counter.

We were put into programs that included four years of science and four years of math. These were the first college prep programs in public schools. On top of a better education, we were encouraged by our teachers to aim for college as a goal in itself. This was the first time when middle class kids were pointed at college and urged to focus on being successful. I don't think I ever heard the terms "give back" or "pay forward." Instead, the idea was that if we studied hard and were successful, we were giving all we needed to give. By being successful, it would raise the boat for all Americans and defeat those godless Commie bastards. My God, what a sound concept. I have been pondering the concept of paying forward and giving back. The currently popular mantra is planned, purposeful giving in all directions as an obligation to society. I just don't get it. Maybe it goes back to my parochial education and being taught the idea of fishing. In today's jargon it would be something like, "if you teach a poor person to fish, rather than giving fish forward, the poor can learn to, 'like totally' take care of his, (oops, his or her) own family." I actually think Bill Gates gave plenty in all directions by being successful. Now he is mostly pissing his money down a rat hole, but if that is what he wants to do, that is his own business. After all, it's his money. It is different when corporate America gives my money to charity. I like coffee and when I travel I used to stop at Starbucks. I say used to because I stopped going to Starbucks and now go to McDonald's for coffee. It is almost as good and much less expensive. The thing that put the final nail in the coffin for me with Starbucks is their giving money to charity campaign. They advertise, "The more you spend the more we give." I don't have a list of who they give to, but I bet it is different than those I would choose. This is presumptuous in the extreme. They are not giving their money, they are giving my money. As I said, I don't care if Bill Gates pisses his money down a rat hole, but I care if Starbucks pisses my money down a rat hole. Just price your product less expensively and then I can give money to those I want to give money to. I also don't like to have to choose between a Tall, a Grande, or a Venti. I used to ask for a small.

It has even reached the point where The Corporation for National and Community Service keeps track of "volunteering." Yes, it is a federal agency. In June 2010, "The Giving Back, and Counting it, Corporation" reported that individuals in the "Twin Cities," gave back an average of 44 hours a year in 2009. I may be a cynic, but I think we all would be better off if they worked more at making money and creating economic wealth. It may be a measure of boredom or bad weather. "Hey Marge, it's too cold to go outside. I don't care if we watch *Fargo* again, so why don't we go over to the Community Center and help the Community Organizers help the Somalis."

The Even More Glorious 1960s: What a Time to Be a College Student

We did not hear about much strife in high school. The first of the civil rights movements was not yet in our consciousness. We only had Germans and Poles and everyone got along reasonably well. Polish kids were good football players, mostly linemen.

The first stirring of change that I remember was the primary election of Jack Kennedy. I had attended Lutheran day grade school. In fact, our town had a fairly large Lutheran day grade school and a very large Catholic day grade school. The public grade school was tiny. These parochial schools were called day schools because there were no boarding students. We all went home at night.

We all went to public high school together. It was sort of forced ecumenicalism with the additional benefit of meeting a whole new set of girls. In my case, Catholic girls. We were even warned about them. I remember Reverend Engle, our minister and de facto head of Evangelical Lutheran Day

School, talking to the boys about sex and Catholic girls, even including the Pope's dibs on any kids. My observation was that such scare tactics had the opposite effect of the one intended.

Kennedy was running against Hubert Humphrey in the open Wisconsin primary. "Open" meant that Republicans and Democrats could vote in either primary. Reverend Engle told us that if Kennedy were elected, the Pope would be running the US. We were not told what that would mean, but by implication it was something we should be concerned about. We weren't. We were more interested in beer and girls. Most of the guys I went to grade school with, including me, dated these Catholic girls when we were "integrated" in high school and vice versa They never mentioned the Pope. We didn't want to bring him up either.

Kennedy beat Humphrey, which put a stake in Hubert's heart, as he was from Minnesota, a sister state. It also put an end to the Catholic issue because Wisconsin was full of Lutherans who voted for Kennedy. Kennedy went on to win the presidency from Richard Nixon. We were about half way through high school and getting ready to go off to college. Life was good.

On April 12, 1961, Yuri Gagarin was launched into space and made a successful return—the space race got even hotter. President Kennedy had been elected the previous fall and he had vowed to win this space race. That meant closing the perceived education gap with the Soviets. New emphasis was put on science and math education. Colleges were supported with federal money and graduate education was supported with National Defense Act money. Talk about a good deal for the early Baby Boomers. First, high school education was beefed up, and then college education was focused on "getting students ready for graduate education." And then, the best of all worlds, federal money was made available for good college graduates, e.g., those with good test scores, to spend four to five more years in graduate school.

We could go to school for twenty years. What a great country we lived in. Even better was the fact that if you taught for a few years, the money they loaned you would be forgiven. Those were the days, my friends.

I decided to attend Ripon College, a small private liberal arts college South-West of Green Bay, Wisconsin, better known as "Title Town USA." It was far enough from home that any parental expectations of going home for weekends would be minimal. It wasn't that home had bad connotations, but the freedom of not answering to anyone and the lure of a new experience had a great feel to it. Like many of us, I had no idea what a major even meant. My parents had not even graduated from high school. I thought I wanted to be a theatre major and a small liberal arts college seemed like a good fit. My father was clear in telling me that he thought going to college meant going to the University of Wisconsin and majoring in Engineering. I did not like this idea, but now I think there was much wisdom in it. I visited a few colleges and decided on Ripon. On top of everything the girl that showed me around campus was dynamite. The college recruiters knew even then how to, so to speak, put their best nipples forward.

College was a soda fountain experience, well actually more of a beer bar experience, as Wisconsin was an 18 year old beer state. A great beer bar, The Spot, was three blocks from campus, making it very walk able, even, stumble able. I could do what I wanted, study what I wanted, and play as hard as I wanted. For many of us, it was more than we could have dreamed about. For a few of us, it was more we could handle and that in a sense is also a good learning experience.

As a freshman in a liberal arts institution, all students faced an array of required courses with a pretty hefty philosophy requirement. The first semester, I enrolled in a religion course that qualified as a philosophy requirement. It was taught by the former football coach, Jerry Thompson. He was so modern he wanted us to call him Jerry. Coach Thompson, sorry Jerry, had retired from coaching and had enrolled in a Lutheran seminary, returning to campus as the college chaplain. I figured that class would be a "tit," after eight years of Lutheran grade school. For some reason, in the early 1960s, we referred to an easy course as a tit. A young female reviewer of this manuscript asked me what that meant. After much rumination, aided by two or three martinis, I concluded that it must have meant easy as in a baby getting milk from a mother's breast. We talked about tits all the time in 1963, but that talk was cheap, mostly boasting.

Coach Thompson, Jerry, told us early in this class that he did not believe there could be such a thing as a "virgin birth." He said it was scientifically impossible. Being more than shocked, I returned to the freshman dorm and worried about it for a bit. How could this be? Reverend Engel had told me it was factual. My roommate, Ron, a Catholic, returned to the room and suggested we go drink beer. I decided there were more important things than virgin birth. What a mind-expanding experience that was and dope had not yet even appeared on the scene. Pot would take three more years.

In addition to taking "Old Testament," I enrolled in Masters of Modern

Drama, taught by Philip Clarkson. It was in his class that a major Boomer marker fell. Marker, as in, where were you when President Kennedy was killed? Class had just started at 1 pm, Friday, November 22, 1963. An out of breath classmate burst into the room shouting that President Kennedy had just been shot. Dr. Clarkson walked to the door, turned and faced us with a serious stage face. As he closed the door, he exclaimed, "The show must go on." And it did.

Since I had Dr. Clarkson for a class and he was directing the play, *Come Back Little Sheba*, by William Inge, I decided to try out for the play. I instinctively understood that if you were in a play you would get an A in a theatre course. It's like coaches teaching classes for athletes. Have you ever heard of an athlete flunking a coach's course? Maybe that is a new definition of a tit course. Dr. Clarkson had an assistant director for the play. His name was Harrison Ford. Clarkson and Ford cast me as the Postman. In addition to being the assistant director, Harrison was the understudy to all the male roles. I have taken great delight over the years telling friends, even new acquaintances, that when I was a freshman in college, Harrison Ford, who was a senior, was my understudy. I doubt he tells the story as often as I do.

These were absolutely wonderful years—I joined a fraternity and lived an Animal House type life for three more glorious years. Some very good teachers inspired me. Then we probably would have said "turned me on." In those golden years, faculty actually taught. Now they do research and most of the teaching is done by graduate students and adjunct faculty.

During the first semester of my junior year I took an economics course from a long time Ripon professor, Dr. Livingston, who had been a Ripon graduate himself. His lectures made more sense to me than anything I had ever listened to. The proverbial light went on. I switched my major to economics. Near the end of my senior year, he asked me what I was going to do beside marry Susan. I told him I was going to go to law school at UW. His reply was, "No, you are going to get a PhD in economics and you are going to go to the University of Virginia to get it." I did what he told me and never regretted it. Rarely do advisors give such straight forward advice these days. It may have something to do with lawsuits.

I was playing hard, learning exciting things, and getting ready for federally supported graduate school. I was elected president of Merriman House, Animal House North. I was sort of the geeky president, as in the movie. The "House" was true to the script before there was a script. Being president gave me a good excuse to return for my senior year a week early. I told my parents that the president, that would be me, was responsible for opening the house, as in getting it ready for the return of the frat brothers. My parents had not been to college and always believed my explanations of what was expected!

Animal House North Scouting Party.

Freshman and transfer students arrived a week early and that was my real motivation. My girlfriend from my junior year had "evaporated" and I wanted first crack (so to speak) at the new women. I met my wife, Susan, who transferred in after two years at a Lutheran junior college that first week.

Those were the days my friends—I knew they would end, so let's stay in school as long as we can. Besides, staying in school might keep us out of the Army. Those who flunked out, like my freshman roommate, were drafted. No lottery numbers, yet.

There were some stirrings of protest. The civil rights movement had started to gain momentum in the South. In March 1964, my sophomore year, Martin Luther King came into my consciousness for the first time. He was protesting the shooting of Jimmy Lee Jackson who had been shot by an Alabama state trooper while participating in a voting registration campaign.

Six hundred marchers, led by the Student Nonviolent Coordinating Committee (SNCC) and the Southern Christian Leadership Conference (SCLC), crossed the Edmund Pettus Bridge over the Alabama line en route to Montgomery. The Alabama State Troopers and local police blocked their way. They ultimately used teargas and billy clubs to turn them around. Over fifty protestors were hospitalized. This riot was on TV and dubbed "Bloody Sunday" by the press. We had a TV in the fraternity house basement and sometimes we even watched the news. The Civil Rights movement was now in our consciousness. On March 21, a successful march on the same route was made with federal protection. A group from Ripon College, with Reverend Thompson, participated in this march. They recently had a 45th reunion of the trip, which was celebrated in the Ripon alumni magazine. I was surprised to see that a (black) fraternity brother of mine was one of the marchers. The next month one alum wrote in and criticized the College for honoring the alums that went with Jerry. He was too old to be a Boomer, much older.

In the early 1960s, we had not yet heard the term African American. I was white and Dave was black. Most of the early Boomers never felt much of a motivation to change; we were not racist, but we also had not yet been bombarded by the concept of political correctness.

I did not remember Dave's going on this protest trip. In retrospect, even more interesting to me is that the fraternity brothers never seemed to think that there was anything out of the ordinary about the black fraternity members we had in Animal House North. As a scout, this was an important observation for the future.

Animal House North had three black members. In insulated rural Wisconsin in 1964, it did not seem anything but ordinary. I can't recall one fraternity rush meeting that any issue of race came up. I guess we were too busy drinking beer to realize we were ahead of our time, perhaps even on the leading edge of integrated colleges. I was surprised to realize when I enrolled at UVA for graduate school that the fraternities did not have black members. Come to think of it, in 1967, there were no blacks or women in the undergraduate College at the University of Virginia. It is important for scouts to understand the indigenous population and its culture.

Many years later, a black colleague told me that the difference between whites in the South and whites in the North was that whites in the South did not mind living with blacks, they just did not want to work with them. In the

North, whites did not mind working with blacks, they just did not want to live with them. I told him about my 1960s fraternity experience and I could not make him believe that I was not making it up.

Protest movements became commonplace and were seen by the swelling number of Boomers in college as a way of getting things done. Some even found the confrontation—well, fun. Maybe some of the same tactics could get us out of Vietnam. Who wants to get shot for reasons we don't understand or worse yet, don't agree with or even care about. Maybe even shot if we agree with the reasons, but aren't interested in the fight. Getting shot seemed like a very bad deal. Vietnam consumed our thoughts in the late 1960s. We were worried about our friends who had been drafted or enlisted and almost everyone knew someone who had been wounded or killed. Shit, we were worried about ourselves being hurt or killed. A fellow pledge class fraternity brother of mine was killed. We all have similar sad stories. Most of us didn't pay much attention to Vietnam before it was "our" war.

Vietnam had actually been with us a long time, but not in our "consciousness," a real Boomer word. President Truman gave military aid to France in 1950, as France was fighting Commie rebels in Indochina. Truman must not have been up on his recent history, as he should have known that the organized French Army, as opposed to the French Freedom Fighters, did not have a stellar record of fighting in the recently completed WWII. The old joke was how did the Nazis take Paris? Answer: "the German Army marched in and asked for a table for 20,000." Later, President Eisenhower considered nuking the Ho Chi Minh led Commies, but, in the end, he backed off and let the French lose at Dienbienbphu. In April of 1954, Eisenhower coined the term domino theory for Indochina. "When you have a row of dominoes set up, you knock over the first one, and what will happen to the last one is the certainty that it will go over very quickly." Think of that. All these years we Boomers blamed the domino theory on that lying bastard, Nixon, not on kindly old Ike. Everybody liked Ike. He even had campaign buttons that read, "I like Ike." Even my dairy farmer grandfather liked Ike, and Grandpa Ed hated Republicans. He was dying of cancer during Watergate and lived much longer than he would have because he was so interested in watching the Watergate Hearings. He had always known that Nixon was a crook and he wanted to see it proven to all Americans. But, he loved Ike. He even had a dog he named Ike. Grandpa Ed must have liked Ike because he won the war and beat Hitler. My grandmother,

Cenayda Amacher was my first teacher. She was the first to tell me that there were Jews in the family woodpile near Bern, Switzerland, yet another reason for their hatred of that bastard, Hitler.

My parents dropped me off at my paternal grandparents, dairy farm whenever they needed a break. This was often. Twins are a test, particularly, twins of different sexes. I was lucky that I drew the Cenayda card. Cenayda had been a teacher in a one-room schoolhouse before she married. She was forced to quit teaching when she married my grandfather because married women could not teach at that time in Wisconsin schools. We've come a long way, baby.

Grandma was the only person I knew who talked about "things." Things like history, politics and books. She is the first person I can recollect who expressed interest in ideas. On a visit in 1971, she told me she was not going to vote because she could not bring herself to vote for George McGovern. She said that even though she had pulled the Democrat lever in every election since FDR, her only choice was to stay home. I knew then that George McGovern was dead meat. He only carried one state—Massachusetts. My friend, Metz, told me he had a similar experience. His staunchly Democrat grandmother told him she could not vote for McGovern. She had seen a picture of him sitting in his hotel room with his feet on the bed, and he had his shoes on!

In 1959, Major Dale Buis and Master Sergeant Chester Ovnard were killed in Vietnam. They were the first two of 58,148 American service men and women killed in Vietnam. This includes eight US Servicewomen. Five nurses were killed in three non-combat plane crashes and two died of disease. Only one woman, 1st Lt. Sharon Ann Lane, was killed in combat. The most striking thing about this statistic is how women have integrated themselves into the combat arms since Vietnam.

Vietnam was always in our thoughts. Nixon took the brunt of this. We did not understand that every President, beginning with Hoover, was involved in Vietnam. Kennedy sent 5,000 Marines in 1962. President Johnson pledged not to widen the war. This was before his election against Barry Goldwater and his use of the TV ad with a mushroom cloud implying that Goldwater would use nuclear weapons. After his election, he increased troops to more than 200,000 by 1965. By the time Johnson left office, troop strength was at 540,000. Maybe it should have been "Tricky" Lyndon.

In April 1965, the SDS (Students for a Democratic Society) held the first large anti-war rally in Washington, DC. The anti-war protests were now in full swing. Protest, with drugs, sex, and rock and roll was fun with a cause. That is not to minimize the commitment, but for many it was great adventure. Have you noticed that when there is trouble with the "authorities," it is always the young throwing the rocks and picking up the tear gas canisters and throwing them back?

Think of the World Trade Organization. Why would anyone protest the WTO Ministerial Meetings? These meetings, in recent years, have reduced tariffs and spread economic growth around the world. Really, the only people in the US who have lost from these meetings are union members. Think how Bill Clinton "triangleized" these union voters. He told them he would support their issues, mostly anti-free trade. They voted for him. And then he became a great free trade President. I don't think they have figured it out yet. This was President Clinton's greatest hour.

Back to the WTO Meetings, there is always trouble. Watch next time. It is great theatre. In Seattle, in 1999, it was dubbed the "Battle of Seattle." Since then there have been riots at every WTO Meeting. Pay attention next time to the ages of the "protesters." There are two groups. First, are the old Trade Unionists. They stand respectably behind the barricades and hold up signs arguing that their artificially high salaries should be maintained by trade barriers being kept in place. Almost everyone understands this and pays no attention to them. They are correct, but most people understand that they are only correct for themselves. In addition, they are very peaceful. They have no intention of being gassed.

They don't have to be gassed because they have plenty of help from know-nothing 20-somethings who don't understand that free trade helps everyone except Trade Unionists in monopolized industries. It makes their salaries higher because consumers are forced to pay higher prices. They are the fools throwing rocks and, in essence, voluntarily gassing themselves.

Why are young people so eager to protest? To be sure they are idealistic, but it is also FUN. You get to act up, get stoned, and if you are lucky you might even get laid, because the female version of these know nothings get excited by young studs playing revolutionary games.

People this age just figure out ways to "make trouble." Years ago, I was a Dean at Clemson University. The capable VP for Student Affairs put it this way. "Sometime between the ages of 18 to 25 young men climb up Fool's Mountain. Our job is to make the journey as 'safe' as possible." For similar reasons, and understanding this, Jim Rogers (*Adventure Capitalist: The Ultimate Road Trip Random House, 2003*) predicted great change in Iran. He is very likely right; there are lots of young Iranians and they seem to be getting sick of the clerical bullshit.

The Go-Go 1970s and 1980s

We should mark the real end of Vietnam as January 21, 1977, when Jimmy Carter, arguably the nicest, and at the same time, most incompetent President of our Boomer Generation, pardoned most of the 10,000 Vietnam era draft evaders. Of course, for those wounded and the families of those killed in Viet Nam, it will never be over. For the other Boomers, Vietnam was over, and as a generation, the first of us were now two years into our 30s.

We next experience Barry Goldwater, oops, Ronald Reagan, and the paring back of big government. Actually, Reagan was taught well by Margaret Thatcher, arguably the greatest politico of the 20th Century. And again, we Boomers were in the right place at the right time. The economy did very well for most of us, and as an added bonus, the Evil Empire came apart at the seams. Reagan turned up the heat on the Commies by developing a Star Wars Defense System. He had intelligence that showed the USSR was tapped out by defense spending and a dysfunctional economic system. It indeed came apart at the seams. He was right.

Unlike Reagan, many Boomers, if not most, don't understand how dysfunctional and brutal these systems were. At the end of the twentieth century, Americans were polled on a number of issues. Boomers overwhelmingly ranked Hitler as the most evil person in the century. For a moment, consider the evilness of some other evil leaders. Using the evilness gauge of the number of their own citizens killed, Stalin, Mao, and Pol Pot all trump Hitler when it came to killing innocent citizens. Like Hitler, both Lenin and Stalin took particular delight in killing Jews, but they were both equal opportunity murderers when it came to killing and working to death citizens they viewed as threats to the regime. Pol Pot probably was the worst killer of the three, if you normalize the numbers killed as a percent of the total population. Mao was no piker in his level of depravity. If you want to go beyond Hitler in terms of evilness, read the *Black Book of Communism* (*Courtois,et.al. ,Harvard University Press, 1999*).

Reagan left office as the great wall tearer downer. This was a monumental achievement, freeing large numbers of Central and East European people who had been sold out by FDR after WWII. We should perhaps be kinder to FDR. If he had not been sick and dying, Stalin might not have hoodwinked him. But he was sick and Stalin did hoodwink him. I am not sure, but I don't think this is taught in schools these days even though most historians agree on it. Teachers who don't read history think FDR was a god. They also take history for teachers, not history for history majors in college.

After Clinton was elected, things returned pretty much to normal. Clinton picked up on the Kennedy tradition in the womanizing department. He just wasn't as good at keeping it undercover, so to speak. Actually, womanizing may not be a bad trait in presidents if it keeps them from focusing on other economic or military activities. There are worse things than having sex with interns. The economic triumph of Clinton was in expanding free trade and keeping the labor unions in check on free trade. If you haven't seen *Commanding Heights,* a great PBS documentary on economics, buy it and watch it—it is a great and fair review of the economy in the last half of the twentieth century—your history.

George H. W. Bush seemed to be a potentially great President. After all, he worked well with Democrats when he was Governor of Texas. Oh, big mistake, most Democrats in Texas are sort of like Republicans.

Markers

When we summarize our Boomer History, the markers on it have to include the triumphs of Dr. Jonas Salk, Dr. Benjamin Spock, Sputnik, the assassination of President Kennedy, Vietnam, the Civil Rights Movement, the Moon Landing (which I missed as I was in Army basic training at Indian Town Gap, Pennsylvania), the invention of the internet, the World Trade Center terrorist attacks, and finally, the great recession-depression of the Bush/ Obama presidencies. The first Black Presidential candidate should have been expected to do well with Boomers and the sheer number of Boomers appears to have tipped the scales. What I mean by this is that I suspect many Boomer Republicans voted for President Obama because it "was time" for a Black President to prove that the US had achieved an integrated society.

I came to this conclusion, in part, because of a "dust up" I had before the election. The future mother-in-law of my wife's favorite second cousin, Grace, was attending an outdoor Labor Day cocktail party with a group of us.

Her future mother-in-law announced that she had voted a straight Republican ticket her entire life, but this year she was voting for Obama. I, ignoring my father's coaching to never discuss religion or politics in public, replied loudly, "THAT IS THE STUPIDIST FUCKING THING I HAVE EVER HEARD." They left. On reflection, and being lectured by my wife about tact (again) I came to the conclusion that many Boomers were going to support Obama for the wrong reason. They were going to vote for him because he was black. It is the only logical conclusion. It also means the second election will have a different dynamic. Susan still thinks I was impolite, a Boomer "disease." I could not stop myself!

Our Present

Presently, we are turning 60 in droves. Our parents, "the Greatest Generation," enjoyed the greatest unprecedented stretch of economic growth in the last half of the twentieth century. Many of us will inherit, or have inherited the bounty of their wartime sacrifice, their hard work, and their great luck in being part of a golden period in American economic growth.

Our present seems bleaker. The economy has tanked. Here again, we are lucky. The real losers are those who expected to retire now. This group is the tail end of the Greatest Generation. They thought they were going to retire rich. They got screwed. Most of us have time before we want to draw on our retirement savings. We are likely to have very high rates of inflation in the future. You can't have the increases in the money supply we are having and the huge deficits without having accompanying high rates of inflation. This will increase the price of real assets. Our home values and other investments will recover when this inflation strikes. That is the appeal of gold. In fact, if you have the stomach for being a slumlord, it would be a good time to become one.

One thing about the present and current problems is that they often go away pretty quickly. The great Swine Flu pandemic of 2009 went away so quickly it didn't become a pandemic—go figure. If we had not been warned about it every sixty seconds, we would not have even known we had a pandemic. Maybe we didn't. When the H1N1 shots finally did arrive, the non-pandemic was over and the government could not even give them away. They are now being destroyed. Did any reporter say on TV that this might be a good example about how good a job government does in medical markets? Even worse, it had happened before and we did not learn any lessons.

In January 1976, an Army private, David Lewis, died on a 50 mile hike at Fort Dix in New Jersey. He had the swine flu. Many more servicemen at Fort Dix tested positively for swine flu antibodies. President Ford held a press conference with Jonas Salk and Albert Sabin. President Ford had just lost the North Carolina Presidential Primary to Ronald Reagan. President Ford promised to increase delivery of a vaccine. He asked the Democrats, who controlled Congress, to spend $135 million to get the job done. The Democrats sped a bill to him, but added $1.8 billion in welfare and environmental spending. Ford signed the bill and announced to the press (incorrectly) that the flu was identical to the deadly 1918 flu.

Many people were vaccinated. It was President Ford's stated goal to vaccinate the entire US population. The flu did not turn out to be deadly, but the vaccine did. MDs joke that many more people died from the vaccine, than from the flu. Some refer to it as the Jerry Ford flu. And don't forget that $1.8 billion in permanent spending.

Our Future

Our medical future looks very good. When I say our future, we are talking in round numbers about our life expectancy. It will continue to creep up as scientific research and medicine solve many of the maladies that come with aging.

Think of the promise of stem cell research. For me, one silver lining to the election of Barrack Obama might be what it might mean for stem cell research. The Religious Right will no longer be able to prevent us from learning the great things that science can do for humankind. Do they really think that God would not be for stem cell research? If they do, "get real," another 1960s phrase. I guess I find it hard to believe that God takes a position on these things. I never felt God took a position on free throws. I was amused when my Catholic friends crossed themselves before attempting a free throw. I thought God had much bigger issues to deal with.

We will likely see programs developed that can address Multiple Sclerosis, Parkinson's disease, and Alzheimer's, among other scourges. My maternal grandfather died from Parkinson's. My twin sister died from MS at age 50, and my mother and father died from Alzheimer's. Alzheimer's will get a lot of attention because of the flood of Alzheimer's patients. It is predicted that the number of Alzheimer's patients will increase by more than 250% in the next 30 years. Again Boomers will drive a social agenda.

I am ready for stem cell research. The God of my childhood was a kindly, you are saved by grace, God. Such a God is not likely to be opposed to solving the medical scourges of our time. If the Religious Right does not want to use the results of this research, they should feel free not to, but, please, someone tell them to stay out of science and the lives of the rest of us. Let their judgmental God prescribe their behavior, but leave me out of it. My God is a Libertarian. I have come to the conclusion that libertarian thought is the operational definition of GRACE. How about this for a deal? I won't tell you that you can't have twelve kids and in return, stay the hell out of my life. Maybe Republicans would be more successful if they would tell these folks to take a hike. If they don't soon, they may never elect another President.

I also expect that we will soon be able to go out in dignity. A future administration will support assisted suicide legislation when it works its way through Congress. Yes, we will be able to choose assisted suicide. This is a great relief for me, as I have been in many discussions with friends when we make pacts to "off" each other at the appropriate time. We all know we won't follow through, if for no other reason, we will have forgotten about it. If we don't forget the promise, we will have forgotten where we put the pistol. And importantly, we would be subject to retribution from "do gooders" who want to dictate our choices.

I think assisted suicide will happen for two important reasons. First, many Baby Boomers are for it. I don't have any friends of my decade who are opposed. And most importantly, we all would take the position that it is fine if you are opposed to it. You don't have to go for it. But even more importantly, it is in the economic interest of our following generations to be supportive. There are no economic losers here. The Religious Right will protest, but they have not led on an issue, ever. Maybe they led on the Crusades. Too bad they didn't follow through on that. If they had, we would not be so worried about terrorism today. They will not win on assisted suicide. It will pass. Economics is on the proponents' side. It will become a pocket book issue.

This suicide shot might even be called a Kevorkian, as in, "tell the nurse, I will have my martini, straight up." You can have whatever you want, even a

Shirley Temple, but I am having a martini. The nurse might ask, "What would you like in tonight's martini?" "My Kevorkian."

I really think assisted suicide or suicide by choice might have become more respectable, more quickly, if Kevorkian had not looked so ghoulish. I saw a rerun of an interview him shortly before he died. He seemed very kindly and sensible.

If you think about it, we treat our dogs and cats with more dignity than we treat our loved ones. My wife and I are on our fifth dog in 43 years of marriage. One of our dogs got killed in a car accident; three of them had to have a doggy Kevorkian. These were some of the saddest moments of our lives. We had to take them into the vet. In one case, with Cinder, you guessed it, a Black Lab, I brought the remains home and Susan and I buried her in the back yard in sight of beautiful Mt. Crested Butte. Things have now become a little bit more humane in that your vet can arrange to have your dog cremated and you can pick her up later. If we treat our pets with so much dignity, shouldn't we demand it for ourselves? We will be taken up on the deal, because there are so many of us, it makes economic sense to grant our wishes. Now, I am not arguing that we should kill old people. I am only suggesting that people who have made it clear that they want to be treated as well as they treated their dogs, should have their wishes respected. A friend once told me that heaven is where all your dogs come running to meet you. I love that idea and I tear up every time I think about it. If I were an actor I could use the thought of it when I had to cry on film. I wonder if Harrison Ford puts this in his mind if he has to "tear up" on camera. Sorry—he doesn't take teary roles.

Economics always trumps religion; always has. The Reformation had more to do with the German princes being pissed off at the high taxes they had to pay the Pope, than with the teachings of Martin Luther. Come to think of it, the German princes financed Luther. Speaking of religion and economics, the main reason the Roman Catholic Clergy couldn't marry was the church did not want any of its assets to be passed on to the heirs of its priests.

For years I have thought that younger generations would resent us when we got older. We will be a problem, a large number problem. You don't have to be a forecaster to anticipate the problems; you can count them now. We already have been born. By the time we reach 66, we will all qualify for full Social Security. We have been paying in since we started work, many of us in our early teens, now it is our time to receive. We will receive more benefits even if we have more income and wealth than those paying into the system. What makes this such a bad deal for younger generations is that there are so many of us. In 1950, there was one Social Security retiree for every 5.1 workers paying into the system (that is, each worker paid for 19.6% of a recipient's SS transfer). By 2007, it had fallen to 3.3—meaning each worker was responsible 30.3% for a retiree; in 2030 it falls to 2.1 workers per retiree. That means each worker paying into the system will be supporting 47.6 % of a retiree's transfer.

Perhaps, we should give each person paying into the system a picture of their recipient, like do-gooder organizations do to get people to adopt starving kids in 3rd World Countries. Workers paying into Social Security could even write to us and we might write back. "Yes, Fred, active worker and Social Security Tax Payer, Susan and I had a great day. We played a round of golf this afternoon, and now we are having a martini while we watch Fox News. Please keep working hard; we will try to play hard and stay healthy so you can support us for ten more years." That is why I originally thought that we would need to be protected in retirement ghettos away from the bounty hunters.

But, I have changed my mind. We have so, socialized, some might say brain washed the young, that they probably won't resent us. The young have become multicultural, social justice seekers for the sake of social justice alone. They probably will consider this just part of the paying forward in a just society, which we discussed earlier. I say PUKE. People with higher levels of income should not get transfers from people who have lower levels of income. That is my measure of fairness. Transfers from the poor to the rich strike me as being unfair, but I am not going to give my Social Security payment or health care transfer away, the cost of good gin has been going up. Also, remember we were forced to pay into what was billed as a retirement program. As Governor Perry has written, it is a Ponzi scheme. He is correct. Politicians have been lying about Social Security for a very long time. Think how much more we will be loved when we turn 66 and become eligible for full Social Security benefits, even if we stay fully employed.

For some liberal Boomers, the idea of receiving Social Security benefits is bothersome. My wife and I spent a recent holiday with an old friend who lives in Austin, Texas, ground zero for liberal think in Texas. She told us she is not drawing her Social Security benefits because she "does not need the money as much as the government does." I tried to talk her into drawing it and giving it to some cause she likes, perhaps even me. I told her that if she took her benefits, cashed the check, and threw the money on the street it would be better spent. For sure, times have changed and the thinking of some of our Boomer friends have what seems to me, wrongheaded ideas. They do not remember why it was so good for us. My wife recently attended her 40th class reunion in Minneapolis. We have a family policy of not attending each other's high school reunions. She subsequently got into a discussion on email with an old friend about Mark Dayton, then running for Governor of Minnesota. That would be the Mark Dayton that is heir to the Dayton store chain fortune. He wants to significantly increase taxes on the rich in Minnesota. It even translated into TV ads during the campaign asking the rich "to chip in to help the state." It later "came out" that he keeps much of his inherited money in South Dakota where taxes are lower.

Shortly after the reunion her classmate emailed her. "We have huge problems in this country right now, from which we may never recover. Because we have sold our souls to China for everyday low, low prices, we may never again see the pinnacle of national achievement. In fact, I have discussed this very subject with several of my more—shall I say—competent and influential friends, some of whom were captains of industry, the consensus is that we may, in fact be on our downward spiral, just like all those who have passed before us, since the dawn of recorded time. Some call it free enterprise; some call it capitalism, some call it the profit motive. But whatever our business model has become is about greed, pure and simple, and it is sowing the seed of our destruction. Because I am who I am and what I am, I will make fun of it. It is all I can do. I am powerless to stop it. It has become a diesel locomotive, chugging headlong to its own destruction. Were I a believer, I would say at this point, God help us. But, I am not. However, there is good news: You have lived a wonderful special life. I know you have enjoyed it. I wish you better news. I have always liked you."

Wow! I was so dumb struck I saved the email. Is it Minnesota? Is it never having taken an economics course in college? Is it naiveté? Is it growing up rich? Is it being raised by Marxist parents? *Stop the World-I Want to Get Off* (Leslie Bricusse and Anthony Newley, 1962). I decided it was a good thing I did not go to her reunions. At mine we talk about the burdensome government we have to deal with. Is the water that different in MSP than rural Wisconsin? I get it—no fluoridation in Wisconsin. My grandmother was right, once again.   It is a good thing we go to our reunions alone. If I had been there, Susan would still be pissed off at me for what I would have said.

There are other issues, and some may even be more troublesome, than the reverse income transfer issue. We might call this the planes, trains, and automobiles problem. First, consider driving. Old people continue to drive in America, and eventually they become less than good drivers, even worse than teenage drivers. We face three alternatives. First, we could make everyone over 70 take an eye exam and a driving test every year to maintain their drivers' licenses. This would not be popular with old folks who have a very high incidence of voting. Another alternative is to greatly expand public transportation and even make it free to seniors. This is a more likely alternative, and since it is "Green" it might be popular with young taxpayers. A third possibility is cars that drive themselves.

Then there are many issues that will need "structural solutions." One that can be seen already is airport crowding and air travel. There are many seniors with money and they travel to see the world and travel to visit their grandchildren. When I was a kid, we traveled across town to visit our grandparents who were sitting on the porch watching cars go by, or later in front of the television. Now they travel. Not only do they travel, they travel on planes AND they carry their bags on. This makes loading and deplaning an issue. If you happen to sit in the back of the plane, it takes 45 minutes to deplane as the old farts struggle with their bags in the overheads. The airlines have it ass-backwards. They should charge for carryon bags and check bags free. They should also make old farts sit in the back of the plane.

The next flying problem is the design of airports themselves. They were designed for people who could walk. They are now filled with so many old people who move around on carts, that it is dangerous to walk. I have wanted to scream at them, "Get your fat ass out of that cart and walk; it would be good for you." In the last year, carts have almost hit me three times. Airports seem to be the only place in America where pedestrians don't have the right of way. I have to admit that I often walk in front of them, purposefully. I also have to admit that I have screamed at them. I have even given some thought to getting hit, falling down, and calling a lawyer on my cell phone en route to the hospital. This would be what we used to call just desserts for my having lost out on the Custer trust fund.

Enough of our general future for now. The next chapter is a guide to taking care of your parents. It could well be the case that as you are starting to care for your parents, your kids will move back home. You have only yourself to blame for this. It was you who made them your best friends. Dr. Spock is not to blame for this either; you are. Dr. Spock wrote that our parents should let kids be themselves that is very different than making them your friends. Making them your friends is co-opting their development. It strikes me this is akin to 18th Century Colonization—family style colonization in the sense that it exploits their own development. We never were best friends with our parents. To paraphrase Kipling, this may well be the new "White Parents' Burden." We will return to kids later in Chapter 7 of this Boomer scouting report.

3

Helping Your Parents Check Out

Dying is not easy, as you know, if your parents have died. If they haven't, you better learn from your friends and me about our experiences. When you turn 60 you are on a path where you will have to help your parents through this difficult time. It will be difficult for you too, but there are some things that you can do to lighten your load. I have scouted this difficult terrain for you.

Hopefully, you have a sister. It seems to me that women are better at this important job. This may seem like a sexist statement, but I have had more than one woman tell me that this process "was one of the best experiences of my life." I call a big horse shit on this as a great experience. This may be part of the caring gene that somehow was not transferred to me. Maybe men don't have this gene or we are more truthful about some experiences. It makes me wonder if gay men are better parental caregivers than straight men. I bet they are. My gay friends have always struck me as caring types. In fact, you can probably get odds on this in Vegas. If you are forced to take this issue on, the first question that should be addressed is where they want to be. NOT, like in your house, or their house, or a care home, but, where, as in Arizona or Minnesota.

My wife's parents were first. They arrived for a month-long summer visit with us in Minnesota. Susan had not seen them in about three months. On that visit to Arizona, she had made the mistake of cooking and cleaning. In retrospect, she thinks she should have stayed away from this task and watched her mother cooking and cleaning. She would have learned then the extent of her decline. You might consider such trips a scouting trip of your own when your parents reach this stage of their lives.

We met them at the small regional airport near our home. At these regional airports you deplane outside, a distance from the terminal itself. They got off the plane on the tarmac and Herman walked slowly, pushing Gladys in a wheel chair, slowly and away from the terminal. We knew then that they were not going home. They were "home."

Her mother was very confused in our house. Each morning she asked me where we kept the jelly. This was a clue to where her mind was. Most of us could become very successful jelly cat burglars because we instinctively know where most people keep their jelly. We could enter any house, steal the jelly out of the "jelly safe," and be out of the house in seconds. I told Susan to put me in "the home" the first time I ask her where we keep the jelly.

We very quickly got the feeling that even though they only came for a short visit, that Herman had come to stay. Proof of this intention was clear when he did not object when we suggested looking for an assisted care facility within a reasonable distance from our house. We enrolled them in the program. We then flew to Arizona to clean out their house and put it up for sale. It sold quickly as it was before the Bush/Obama depression. This whole process would have worked much more smoothly if we had discussed much earlier what they wanted from their former home. From mementos to furniture to clothing, we had to make these decisions for them. This is not easy. There are piles and piles of boxes and more than likely, you will throw some treasures away. They will profess not to care about what you keep and what you dispose of. Later they will be upset about the loss of treasures you threw away. Have this discussion now about where they want to live and the disposition of their things early on. The sooner you do this the easier it will be and importantly, you will have more time to do it in an orderly way.

It was then my turn. I did not see it coming, even though I had witnessed one of the issues from the sidelines. My twin sister is a case study of how the system can go awry. Her multiple scleroses had progressed to the point that she was curled up in a fetal position and could not communicate. It was a very sad state. Several times, she contracted raging infections and was transferred to a hospital. The question of treatment would arise. My father would always decide to treat the infection, only for her to return to her unresponsive state. She had a living will with the provision that no methods should be used to keep her alive. My father was the decision maker. He was unable to make these hard choices. The major lesson here is that the decision maker has to be someone who can make the decisions that the dying person wants. I wish, in retrospect, that I had taken on this role for her. Her wishes were not followed. Most of the doctors will hold out hope. And worse, some clergy are opposed to letting, or "helping" someone die.

In a quite different example, when my 94-year-old paternal grandmother had suffered a stroke and was dying, the family was called to be there. My very sensible aunt, who was the designated power of attorney, decided that her mother should only be kept comfortable. The doctor agreed. The minister tried to talk her out it, unsuccessfully. That is the type of person who should have the power of attorney someone who won't change the wishes of the patient. The lesson here is that if you, the care giver, can't follow the wishes of the care needer, don't take the job. Likewise, if you are setting up your own care, don't choose some pussy for the power-of-attorney designee, someone who can't make the hard decisions. Maybe the market will solve this problem. Third party agents might emerge who can take this important task over for families that are too close "to close."

Money issues are always present and will likely be even more important in the future. As Baby Boomers, this is our first experience with a serious recession. We aren't as rich as we thought we were. But believe me, your parents are much poorer than they thought they would be and you thought they were. This is even more the case if they retired to Florida and Arizona. Their house is not worth what they thought it was worth and worse, they will be reluctant to tell you the state of their finances. They took care of you so get ready to pay up. Paying up is the easy part. Spending time is the costly part. This part is made more difficult by the fact that most of us don't live close to each other anymore. That would make a title for a country song. Maybe it is.

First, force your parents to be frank with you about their financial status. This, in some sense, is a financial outing. The earlier you have this discussion the better. After you get this done, you need to decide if you need to get control of their money. My parents got swindled out of their money before we were aware of it, so we learned from this. We told my wife's parents that if they gave us control over their money, we would take care of them, even if, or when, their money ran out. Your parents may surprise you by being very happy, even relieved, to buy into this deal. Unfortunately, it is not a good deal for you; it could bite you in the ass, even if it is a caring, well intentioned proposal. And there is self-interest in it, as they will run out of money much sooner if you don't get control of it. People are living a long time and it is going to get longer.

You have to get control of everything that is controllable. Get power of attorney over their financial matters and their health decisions. These are usually called, "Durable Power of Attorney for Health Care" and "Durable Power of Attorney for Finances." This can be difficult. They still think in the back of their minds that you can't be trusted. Your mother remembers when she found sticky socks in the laundry, weed in your jeans, and rubbers in the glove compartment. You have to be tough here. Don't be the responsible party if you won't or can't call the shots. You will also need a living will for them. This is usually called in lawyerese, a "Medical Directive."

The next issue to be frankly discussed is: burial or cremation? If they have plans, you are in luck. This is a sensitive, tricky issue. If they like the idea of cremation, one of your jobs has been made much easier. Cremation is easier in that all the arrangements can be arranged and paid for before they are needed. The provider then takes over at exactly the most difficult time, even if you have not arrived on the scene. Some will want to be buried to be near loved ones. There is no harm in telling them they can be cremated and still be buried near loved ones. It is true. If they have religious problems with cremation there is nothing you can do about it. The desire to be buried near loved ones is strong a one. It must be that we all saw Wilder's *Our Town* (1937) too many times.

It was easy for me on this issue. My parents had been thinking ahead because of my twin sister's MS. They realized that she would probably precede them in death so they were thinking about it. They told me they all wanted to be cremated. I expect my sister told them that is what she wanted. They even brought the idea up, way before their health became an issue. I jumped at the idea and bought them spaces in a columbarium that the church they attended built. A columbarium is a bit like high class post office boxes in a garden setting. I bought three—one for my sister and two for them. I gave the memorial boxes to them as a Christmas present. I referred to it as Our Columbarium. They liked it. It was the right size and the right color and it was a tax deductible donation to the church—Bingo, a gift that gave a little back. That is my definition of giving back. My father, the last of the four to die, later expressed concern about where Susan and I would be "forever." I told him we would squeeze in. That made him happy.

The next step in the plan is Power of Attorney. It can be confusing because you want Power of Attorney over everything. You need control of medical needs and decisions, including wills. You also need financial control. Go see a good lawyer and get it all done at the same time and make sure it covers all contingencies. I suggest you don't do it yourself on the computer—you may well find out later that some important component is missing. Everyone signs all documents, with lots of witnesses. Take them to a print shop and have lots of copies made. You will need lots of them and you need to have them in your briefcase, as you will never know when you have to fly in for decisions. Fax them to the hospital. Keep the originals safe and secure in a safe deposit box.

Then prepare a list of all the medication they have been taking. The medicine cabinet will be full of old and new medications they have been taking and forgetting to take. They may even be taking old prescriptions that they have been hoarding. They may not even be able to read the printing on the bottles. If they go to a hospital with you or by ambulance in your absence, you will be asked by phone by the receiving nurses about all these drugs. It will be a mess. MDs are first and foremost prescribers. It is harder to get these records from the pharmacy or other medical providers than you think. Do it before you need it and keep it with you in your briefcase and a copy at their house. It might even be a good idea to place a copy in a conspicuous place, maybe even taped to the medicine cabinet somewhere where the emergency team will see it.

Next, go see the burial folks. This can be a traditional mortuary or a cremation firm. They are very helpful, and they can set up everything in advance. You will need information and you will need pictures, and copies of their vital papers like birth certificates. This is pretty easy, as you needed most of them for the care center. You will need all this stuff eventually so find it before you need it. Be diplomatic. You don't need to tell them that you are doing it.

Since we Baby Boomers moved around so much since we left college and many of our parents moved South in retirement, there is a very good chance that you will be at some distance from one another. Your parents will likely, at some point, need assisted care. Start to look for it before you need it. Spend time on this and find a place they might like. If the need jumps up at you unexpectedly, you can discuss it with the hospital social worker. The social worker can help you a great deal. In my case, a social worker put me onto an assisted care facility within six hours of the "advice" from the doctors that my parents should not go home as they were not capable of caring for themselves. My experience was that these people are informed and very helpful. I took the one that helped me a dozen roses the next day.

I found the people who staff these assisted care facilities to be helpful and caring, a great help, often in trying circumstances. Your parents will not like them, and they may tell you about problems with the care. This may be true in some cases, but my experience was that the staff was very professional. Your parents will tell you that the staff has stolen everything that they themselves have lost or misplaced or you threw away. The truth is that your parents should not have much stuff with them that anyone would want to steal. If someone might want to steal it, don't take it to the facility. Don't leave money around. Get them a credit card that comes to your address, so you can monitor their expenditures. I have a friend that discovered too late that his mother was addicted to the shopping network with her second bedroom full of cheap stuff that she did not even want. She just ordered it. She did not even remember ordering it. She had not even opened the packages.

The folks that work in these care centers do a great job under very trying circumstances. I hope they will be rewarded in the next life as they don't seem to be rewarded in this life, either financially or by the people they serve. Many of the patients are not often appreciative. But then they are old, lonely, scared and cranky. I was, however, often shocked to see the way that some relatives of "inmates," a term my father used to refer to himself, beat up on the caregivers. On my visits, I always tried to touch base with the caregivers and thank them for who they were and what they did, specifically as it related to my parents. They made my life easier, much better than it would have been without them.

It will likely be the case that your parents will begin to show signs of dementia. The doctors told me that there are not many differences between Alzheimer's disease and other forms of dementia. That may be the case, but it appeared to me that Alzheimer's moved faster. Maybe that is a good thing, or is it the other way around? I forget.

In this whole experience, I did not understand a few of the regulations the staff imposed on the inmates. The most curious prohibition was in food preparation. It concerned salt consumption. In the dining hall, they restricted salt intake by not having salt on the tables. As a result, many of the residents did not think the food tasted good. Hey, these folks are dying, let them have salt. My father complained, mostly about the food. I told him it was my way of getting even for the shitty food I had to eat in college. I wanted to buy him a saltshaker and a supply of salt, but he declined. I suspect when we Boomers get to this stage of life, we will rebel and carry our own salt with us at all times. Dope in the right pocket—salt in the left pocket.

My parents were both smokers when I was a kid. I offered to go buy them some smokes. Smoking is really a social exercise. Even more so now that it is regarded as antisocial. When I was a dean at Clemson the Provost's secretaries marveled at how short my meetings were with my boss, the Provost. We were both "closet smokers." I would go to his office and he would say, "let's talk on the porch," where we had a smoke. The business was always concluded favorably and quickly. I suspect that if Speaker John Boehner and President Obama sneaked away and shared a "smoke" they might get business done more quickly. Excuse me, I take that back, I do not want them to get "things" done more quickly. I don't want them to get things done, period.

I made this offer to buy some smokes for my parents as I had observed a group hanging out smoking in the garden and sometimes in a corner of the parking lot. They were a band of rebels. They were joking, even those in wheel chairs. They seemed to be having a lot more fun than the others. I suggested that it might be fun for them to join this group. My parents looked at me like I was crazy. I vowed on the spot that I would take up smoking menthols (again) when I turn 75, no next week.

Visiting your parents can be a strange and confusing experience for you and them. Sometimes they will say and do the strangest things, sometimes funny and sometimes shocking. Many times shockingly funny. They might be confused about who you are. You might even learn some deep bloodline secrets. It is such a role reversal. Art Linkletter could have done a show, "Parents in assisted care say the damndest things."

If you are lucky, as I was, you will have some friends in the distant place your "incarcerated" (my father's term) parents live. I had the luxury of staying with one of mine on caregiver visits. I have a friend, Metz, in nearby Tempe. I eventually even left clean clothes and supplies at his house. These breaks with friends were fortunate. They greatly assisted my mental health and helped me see the humor involved in the turmoil.

The real issues start when your parents edge nearer death. Even though you have Power of Attorney over life and death matters and a Living Will, you will have to diligently enforce the wishes they made to die with dignity. When the time comes it will take true diligence to enforce their wishes. Don't take this important task on if you are not up to it. I know I am repeating this advice. This is purposeful as it is critical.

My mother had severe Alzheimer's for about a year. She "graduated" from the Assisted Care Unit and was moved into the Alzheimer's Center in the same building. If you have two parents in this situation, an assisted care facility with an Alzheimer's unit is a good idea. My father was able to visit her every day. It gave him a mission in life. This went on for about ten awful months. I flew out to check on them every other month, or so. She eventually had an episode that sent her to the hospital. I immediately got on a plane to get involved. Before I got there she slipped into a coma and was moved to yet another care facility. It was sort of a pre-school for hospice. When I arrived, my father was sitting at the end of the bed. She was dying and had no idea what was going on. A nurse took me aside and told me that in the morning they were going to start physical therapy. I said "**NO**, you are not." We had conflict. I said that I have Power-of-Attorney over health decisions and she is not going to have therapy. The nurse looked at me as though I were demonic.

It should not be this hard to die. The therapy, to be sure, was no longer relevant. That final night my father refused to let me take him back to his assisted care facility. I got the feeling he sensed the end and wanted to stay. I thought it was a good idea, but his insistence on staying still makes me tear up. It was the first time that I saw him show affection—Germans, you know. After she died, I returned and took him to his now very lonely "home."

It was a similar story with him, only I did not get there before he died. He went back to the assisted living center after my mother died and he declined quickly without her to focus on. He developed dementia and then finally fell and broke a bone in his foot. He was taken to an emergency center. The doctors called me and told me they were going to operate. I said no. They argued with me. They moved him to a Care Center. When he arrived, a very caring female doctor called me to tell me that he arrived and was being kept medicated. She did not lobby for further treatment and told me that he would not live through the night. He died 60 minutes later. NOW, why would you operate on a broken foot of a man who is dying? There are some economic incentives here, but I choose not to dwell on them. I must admit that I worry about MDs owning care centers. It's that ugly incentive thing and related to occupancy levels.

My experience was that female doctors were more understanding and sympathetic of the decisions that had been made and were being enforced by a family member. They had less of an ego. I guess. This seemed so universal I have had trouble understanding it. Maybe it proves that female doctors are less godlike, or more compassionate. A doctor friend who read a draft of this chapter told me that most female doctors are mothers and their mothering skills come into play.

Good luck with this "great experience" if it falls in your lap. AND, get with the planning before it does.

4

Health Issues

We Baby Boomers have been turning 60 since 2006. There is a huge group of us and we have significant health issues. Most of us Boomer men don't talk about them. Let's get down to these issues. They hit you directly—some of them in your privates. And let's get down to real issues, not pussy issues like knee and hip replacements. These joint replacements are in part, sometimes to a very large part, self-inflicted. You really weren't that good. The team could have gone on without you. Does anyone but you even remember the record? Even more importantly, they say the replacements will make you feel better. You will be a better person; spring will be back in your step. For those of you who dived out of a fourth floor dorm window your freshman year with a rope around your ankle, you deserve it. These may have been our "Glory Days" (thanks Bruce), but they weren't as "glory-full" as we remember.

It seems to me that the only downside to a knee (or hip) replacement is that if you want to know the weather forecast, you will have to tune into the weather channel. Don't get me wrong, I have nothing against replacing joints, but that is a benefit of being a Boomer, not a cost of growing older.

"I Can See Clearly Now"

The big C, not cancer, cataracts. Cataracts are rites of passage. My internist, Dr. Gary Reed, often said that he hoped I got cataracts because if I did not, it would mean I died from something else first. Cataracts sneak up on you. You need reading glasses. The sun is bothersome when you are in it. Headlights from oncoming cars cause you to divert your eyes. If you live in the North, the snowmobiles coming at you in the ditch on your side of the road will confuse you. Colors seem less vibrant, but then you don't notice that. One day you will be driving in a strange city and the elevated road sign will be between you and the sun. The sign will be one black mass. And you, old man, will be lost. It happened to me on Interstate 35 in downtown Kansas City and I was really lost, pulling a U-Haul trailer on the way to my second home in Minnesota, planned for retirement.

Get yourself to a respected ophthalmologist at a good hospital. You could go to a physician who owns his own clinic and advertises on radio sports talk if you want. Suit yourself. It's that ugly incentive thing again. I also want the operation done in a hospital in case I faint or have a reaction to the anesthesia, or even worse, the ophthalmologist faints. These guys are great. They look you over, put you out and a few days later you even see vibrant colors again. These doctors actually make you better. They don't slow the spread of some hateful thing in your body, and they don't lecture about changing your life style. They make you better. If your kid is thinking about going to medical school, tell her to look into this specialty; you actually make people better. When your patients come to see you for their yearly check up, they are even are happy to see you. They also don't have very many emergencies. This should be a specialty that is crowded. Fathers let your daughters grow up to be ophthalmologists.

Cataract surgery is a new lease on life, with very little maintenance. I return every year for a checkup. My ophthalmologist, Dr. Wayne Bowman, is an interesting guy and it is always good to see him and catch up. My wife and I go the same day, making it a family outing with a tax-deductible dinner. Yes, we make the appointment late in the day and have about 60 miles to travel so we get mileage and food deductions on tax forms. Also, with two, the person whose eyes adjust from the dilation the most quickly, can drive.

About every other year, Dr. Bowman schedules me for a GAK, a procedure that cleans the Yuk that has clouded the inside of the lens. It is not called a GAK because it is Yuk cleaner, but I forget the technical stuff. The bottom line is that it doesn't hurt and it makes you see well again. Man-oh-man, what a great medical specialty and these docs never get body fluid shot all over them. Well, I guess almost never.

There is a correlation between cataract issues and prostate issues. Of course, we all know that from the barrage of TV commercials for Flomax. They warn us over and over that if you are male and are having to pee too often, you should consider Flomax. But if you are taking Flomax and are considering cataract surgery, be sure to tell your physician.

So let's get this clear: Cataracts and Prostate issues are correlated to age. This is your scout telling you to get a physical.

On one trip to visit Dr. Bowman, he motioned me to come into his office before it was my turn. He introduced a man who was a fellow physician at Parkland Hospital. He then asked his colleague to tell me his story and departed to meet with a patient. My new friend told me he was an intern at Parkland in the fall of 1963. On November 22, he began a rotation as the head of the emergency room at 8:00 am. The Parkland emergency room is less than a mile from Dealey Plaza. Shortly after lunch on his first day they rolled in the President of the US with most of his head missing. It was not possible to save his life. He told me that he never again was nervous practicing medicine.

The Other C: The Joy of Kegeling

Yes, Cancer: Prostate Cancer. One in two men will have some prostate issues and symptoms by the age of 50. Yes 50. Yet most of us do not talk about it. Prostate issues are the common denominator of the "senior" male. It does not discriminate, although a black friend from college days told me that there are more psychological issues for a black man with prostate cancer; must have something to do with self image. That is really too bad. They are serious enough issues for white men.

It is a good idea to have a physical every year. It is amazing what your internist can tell from a blood test. My internist cannot only tell me how many martinis I drink each night, but last year he knew that I had changed from an olive to a twist! He also told me his grandfather always said, "A drunk is someone who drinks more than I do!"

As part of this comprehensive blood and urine analysis, your doctor will also measure your PSA, Prostate Specific Antigon. As bad as prostate cancer is, you don't want to be surprised by it. Some men skipped having prostate tests because they were uncomfortable; a strange choice of words, considering a doctor put his fingers up your ass. Get over it. Dying of cancer is worse than a little discomfort and it could be a lot more embarrassing. The PSA tells a lot, but about 10% of prostate cancer patients have normal PSA. That is why the PSA test and the old DRE are best. Some doctors skip the older DRE. There is NO excuse for not having it done, unless you would like to die and are too much of a pussy to commit suicide.

Recently, there have been news reports that "too many" PSA tests are done by doctors. I call a big horse shit on that. How can more information be better than less information? What matters is what one does with the information. Go to a urologist you trust or even better, one your internist recommends, and ask questions.

Also, before you go for your tests get some terminology straight. It is prostate NOT prostrate. The only connection between these two words is that if you don't get your prostate checked regularly, you might be permanently prostrate sooner.

In my case, my PSA was about .1 to .15 for years. It then crept up to 2.1 to 2.8 for a few years before it shot up to 6.9 in late 2007. Dr. Reed sent me to see a urologist, Dr. Claus G. Roehrborn. I should have guessed he was a real German as his staff actually pronounced my German name correctly and this is rarely the case. He was very sure of himself; in fact, he told me he was perfect. Frankly, that was fine with me. I certainly did not want an imperfect surgeon. I scheduled the biopsy and watched. Believe it or not, you get to watch the probe on the journey to the center of your fountain, the source of all those gallons and gallons. Claus told me during the process that my prostate was very large, but smooth, so it might not be cancerous. This was a Wednesday.

On Friday, friends arrived from out of town and we decided to have lunch and margaritas at a new local high end Mexican, yes high end, restaurant in downtown Fort Worth. Sometimes high end Mexican restaurants are called Spanish restaurants in Texas. I was on my second margarita when my cell phone rang and I left the bar area as it was very FUERTE. I went into the bathroom and Claus's nurse told me I had cancer. That is a bad message to receive anytime, anywhere. Wait; maybe a bar is a good place. I went back and reported to all. Our friends offered to go home. We asked them to stay and spend the weekend getting drunk. My wife, Don, and Ginny, helped me drink the horrible thoughts away. Claus called the next day (Saturday) and apologized that the nurse had called to tell me. He had been out of town and had wished to call me. My God, he is perfect and that was a classically perfect move. It was fine with me that she called. Claus is classically German, has the bedside manner of all my uncles in Wisconsin when I was a kid. It was not off putting to me. But, I'm probably still numb from dealing with all those uncles. The nurse delivered the undeliverable news in a soft pleasant, non-German manner that was fine with me. After all, how can you deliver this news, well, nicely?

So what's next? You would think as common as this is, we would all have some idea about the next step. Hardly any of us do, because we don't talk about it. I had the advantage of a friend my age who had gone through the experience about a year earlier. He, like me, is an academic that I first met at my first teaching gig in Boomer-Sooner land almost 40 years earlier. He is very thorough and got several opinions before his treatment. I phoned him. He informed me about the basics and I learned from my first consultation that there are three basic options with some sub options:

1. Active Surveillance (watchful waiting)
2. Radiation
    A. Brachy therapy
    B. Nuclear "seeds" planted in one's prostate
    C. External Beam Radiation (you can have partial surgery)
        a. IMRT
        b. Proton
3. Surgery
    A. Open Radical (lymph node dissection)
        a. Retropubic
        b. Prostatony
    B. Laparoscupic Prostatectomy
        a. Pure
        b. Robotic Assisted da Vinci

Now do you understand why I was satisfied to have found a perfect urologist? There is no way you can understand this medical jargon. My friend's research journey had led him to believe that the da Vinci is the best means of making you cancer free. If you are old, you have a fourth option, nothing; you are going to die from something. But if you have a life expectancy of more than ten years, and they can give you your life expectancy given your other health factors, only total removal means you might die from something else. Hear this: prostate cancer is not a death sentence. But, it is a profoundly life changing experience.

Since I was 62, I went to my pre-op meeting with Claus knowing I was going to opt for Dr. da Vinci. Dr. Roehrborn's reaction was "that is the correct decision, but only you can make it." I was given a reprint of a publication he had written in *European Urology*, 42006. It was entitled, "Laparoscopic and Robotic—Assisted Radical Prostatectomy: Critical Analysis of the Results." Now that was some interesting reading. I decided I would not agonize over a decision that I could not understand. It's robotic assisted radical prostatectomy for me. Doctors and friends I trust recommend it and I don't have enough time left to attempt to understand it. I just don't like seeing radical in the title. Let's get the "nut cutting," so to speak, over with.

Now the da Vinci robot is an interesting piece of equipment—it is big and the surgeon is not near you—so much for MD/patient relationships. It seemed to me that you could be in Anchorage or on the moon, and your surgeon could be in Dallas, or vice versa.

My neighbor, Gayle, once sold penile implants. This makes her an expert on "wiener issues." Gayle also is a fan of TV's "Grey's Anatomy," which my wife also likes. I had never watched it, but she insisted that I watch the final show of the 2009 season. My wife had TiVoed it. TiVo should get many votes for the best invention of this past decade. It puts you firmly in control of TV entertainment but, back to Grey's Anatomy. It was titled, "Here's to Future Days; Now or Never." You should watch it before surgery, it will give you confidence. It shows da Vinci at work and it was impressive.

Let's go; surgery is scheduled to be in 38 days. Claus tells me that when the prostate is entirely removed you will no longer ejaculate. The prostate isn't there; there will be nothing left to produce the ejaculate. No more gallons and gallons, as we described it in the day. In other places, I have learned guys said, "buckets and buckets." Same concept. He explained that he would try to preserve the nerve, so that I could have the ability to have an erection. I could still have the sensation of orgasm without the nerve, but the nerve is necessary for erection. Wow—easy decisions—right? I would also have the sensation of ejaculation; even though it would be a dry fire exercise, so to speak, meaning no wet spots. Claus went on to say that each time a patient returns for a check-up, he gets a PSA exam, the MD, he or she (I actually met a female urology intern on a recent visit—didn't matter) will monitor the status of incontinence, and they will monitor erectile function. He explained that they would ask me to compare my erections to "teenage" erections. This should have been pause for concern. I had not had a teenage erection for at least fifteen years. Shit, that is wishful wet dreaming. Not since I was a teenager. Driving home, I had visions of walking down the hall of old Medford High with a book in front of me hoping not to burst the seams out of my pants.

Before surgery is a good time to start your Kegel Exercises. Most men have never heard of Kegel or Kegel exercises, but most women, particularly those who have had children, know Kegel. Ask them for advice. They will think back about when they had the issue, and how you were not that sympathetic. They might find the turnabout somewhat amusing and will surely be more supportive than you were. Women are like that.

Kegels are pelvic muscle exercises. In men, the pelvic muscle supports the bladder and the rectum. If it gets weak, you leak, yes, leak, as in taking a leak in your pants. Your wardrobe will require dark pants. What a life change. A whole new wet spot issue. You will find your supply of clean khaki pants remains untouched, but you and only you can solve this issue. In fact, when you get back to your khakis, you are on the road to recovery.

You should Google Kegel exercises and get to work before your surgery. You will be glad you did, as it will allow you to get past the diaper thing more quickly, yes diaper thing. There is nothing else you can do to solve this leakage issue.

The more Kegels you do, the more quickly you will get over the fear of pissing in your pants. You can even learn how to do them before surgery. A good time to knock off a lot of them is when you are sitting down to pee. Yes, sitting down. You will be sitting down to pee after surgery as you will have to remove your shorts and slip down the diaper—sorry, pad. And it is just easier to do this sitting down. If you don't sit down, you will spray all over the floor even more than before surgery. So take advantage of the opportunity and Kegel. This is good practice, as you can develop your new techniques by stopping and starting your pee stream.

Day 1, Surgery. My wife and I arrive at Parkland University Hospital University of Texas. It's 8 am. We are admitted to pre-surgery about an hour later. Thirty minutes later our best friend, Patricia, arrived to lend her moral support. Now you know she is a best friend, because who else comes to your prostate surgery, either your best friend or your worst enemy. Susan and Patricia had not met Claus, so they were introduced. I was getting some pre surgery drugs when Dr. Reed stopped in to see how I was doing. For those of you who dozed off, Dr. Reed is the internist who first noted my high PSA. I bring him up because his visit convinced me that there are caring MDs and well run hospitals. He had actually been informed of the day and time of my surgery, kudos to UT-Southwestern hospital and Dr. Reed. It was getting close and I started to tear up. Why? Hard to explain because I wasn't afraid of the surgery, I didn't think I was going to die. But I knew deep down inside that my life was going to inalterably change. No one had laid it out, but I knew it in my bones, maybe in my boner, for sure there were going to be no more gallons and gallons. This is life changing surgery.

Surgery went well and I was back in the room about 2 pm. Susan and Patricia were in the room waiting. I don't remember much about this, but they told me later they had met with Dr. Roehrborn and he had informed them that he had been perfect. And the surgery had been perfect. Bravo, as I said before, I want my surgeon to be perfect.

My first recollection is coming somewhat alert in time for the overtime of the Kansas-Louisville National Championship game. I was out of surgery but hooked up to a Morphine drip, the good stuff. I know the game was on, but I had to read sports magazines to know much about the game. This is a bit like the Beach Boys having to hire historians to teach them what happened in the sixties, but because of different drugs.

Susan and Patricia went to dinner (finally) and I dropped in and out of drug-assisted sleep. God, that's good stuff. I finally came around a bit about 3 am and Susan was sleeping in the room. Susan rang the highly efficient night nurse who asked if I needed anything. I opted for more drugs. I also asked for coffee, but he would not give me both, and the drugs were the best alternative. I could have as much coffee as I wanted when I got home.

After breakfast, Susan and Patricia had me walking the halls, pulling my urine bag on a roller type setup. My gown kept revealing my privates and the urine bag, but I really did not give a shit, and I am a modest guy. After lunch, it was decided that I could go home. But first, we, and that meant Susan, Patricia, and about four female nurses, had to give and have lessons in urine bag care and maintenance. There we are, six females learning the ins and outs of my catheter, weenie, and urine bag. Leave any modesty on the doorstep.

Modern medicine is something. Major surgery and I am going home with a total pre-op and post-op of 30 hours.

These are the notes that Patricia made from that "instructional meeting," I don't know why I kept them:

> Big bag for night or long car ride
> Lay it on the floor (for gravity drainage)
> Wash it out with vinegar and warm water
> To change bag keep end up. Just push on it to connect

For extension push rubber tip onto bag connection
Watch out for extension
Drain by pushing blue tab
Drink a glass of liquids an hour plus one liquid with meals
No heavy lifting, nothing more than 10 lbs.

Patricia also read all the "Patient Instructions: Care of the Foley Catheter." Instructions like "while you have an in-dwelling catheter, (sounds nicer that a tube up your best friend), you should observe the flow of urine. But if this becomes problematic, please contact the clinic." I hate the word problematic when it is being applied to Robo, my best and oldest friend.

It is wonderful to get home and get in your own bed even if you are hooked up to a tube in the most private place you live. Once we got home I got in my own bed and felt safe. We had a great dinner. One tip, do not eat asparagus until you are off the catheter.

The next day we rigged up a cloth book bag to hold the plastic pee bag. This bag was not a Geenie grocery bag, but a similar concept hooked with some straps over my shoulder so I could drag it around off the floor when I walked. The bag was a conference give away that Patricia had been given at a shrink conference, since psychology is her profession. The irony of the source of the bag was not lost on me. This distance and height thing allowed the bag to fill unobstructed.

This drill of catheter and bag went on for eight days. I pretty much stayed in the house, as I was not enthralled with being a bagman. You really don't want to be out and about. About two months after my surgery I was waiting at a Starbucks for a business meeting when an old guy, older than I, came in for a coffee dragging a urine bag. It is not a good sight. My advice is, stay home until you get the catheter out. Think of someone other than yourself, SHIT, think of yourself, have some self-respect.

Day 9: Catheter comes out. It was my first post-op check up and catheter removal. The physician's assistant, Brad, and the nurse got hosed down, even though they knew enough to try to stay out of the way. They told me to bring pads to this check up, so I had some with me.

It is time for the diapers or pads. I thought of them as diapers, but my wife insisted that I call them pads. The first shock you will have is when you go to the supermarket to buy your diapers, sorry, pads. They are in the row marked: "Incontinence Products," in big letters. The first surprise is that there is a whole row of them. I had never even noticed the row and it was a huge display. Now I watch and have observed that people slip in and out of this display. About a quarter of it was for men. My first reaction was, "who buys all this stuff?" My next reaction was why couldn't they put these products in plain brown wrappers like they used to do with Kotex, then no one would know you were buying them. Come on. I knew what my mother was buying when I was eleven, ok, more like twelve.

Since these male incontinence products do not come in plain brown wrappers you will be a little embarrassed to be buying them. At least I was. Then it dawned on me. Here is the solution. When you are checking out, tell the cute young thing that you are buying them for your father, and ask her if you can bring them back if you didn't get the correct ones. You forgot what brand he asked you to pick up for him, clever, huh?

These modern pads are relatively small and they fit in your jockey style shorts pouch. Boxers or "jigglies," as I have always called them, are going to be out for a while because you need a place to snuggle the pad into. There are no straps, like old style Kotex. It is an amazing technology. The pads capture the pee and don't release it. You can't even wring it out. Just believe me; you don't need to try it. Again we are the lucky generation. "Veee hafe zee technology." No one will notice that you have them on. They work, but you still will be afraid to wear khakis. This khaki fear will last for about a year, as you will be convinced that you are going to leak through them and look like a 60 year old man who just pissed in his pants. Dr. Roehrborn told me on a follow up visit that he smiles to himself when post- prostate surgery patients show up for checkups in khakis. It shows him they have conquered the incontinence issues and have regained some confidence. You have to work hard on this. It is like all exercise programs. Some men have told me that years after surgery they still have some leakage issues. These are the Kegel slackers. Actually, Brad, the physician's assistant, told me that this is a little harsh. Some men don't regain continence regardless of the number of Kegels they do. I am glad I did not learn this until after I had regained continence. If you work hard on your Kegels you will even be able to sleep nude again.

Damn it, you might even consider starting Kegels now as part of your "gym" workout. It couldn't hurt. And the probability is high that you will need them. Even better, no one will know you are doing them. They are a stealth exercise. Just do it. You can even do Kegels when you are driving—it is much safer than texting and you will get a new measurement standard. As in, "how far is the nearest 7-11?" "Go 12 Kegels down this road, turn right at the first intersection and it will be 15 Kegels on the right side."

I came to the conclusion early on that some of the sensation of peeing in your pants is what I called "phantom peeing." You are working so hard on your Kegels and regaining control that you think you are peeing on yourself. Friends have told me they had the same sensations.

Day 18—it is time for me to teach my first course—Economics for MBA students. It is a three hour marathon. I wear black pants, my trusty pad, and two pair of jockeys—a new definition for a double bagger. It felt like it is my first step for mankind.

Day 23—it is my first time back on an airplane—three hours DFW to MSP. I got upgraded and an aisle. Whew. Dark pants, I double bagged. I really mean padded. Only two martinis; after all it is a 6:30 am flight. No issues. I only need to use the rest room on arrival in MSP. First flight no problems, second step for mankind.

But here is a revelation. I go to the public rest room in the Lindbergh Terminal at MSP and approach the urinal. NO, it's not the infamous, senatorial rest room at Lindbergh. That one is in the main part of the terminal, I am nearer the gates. I know the infamous one as the shoe shine guys were directing people to it shortly after "the senatorial incident."

In order to use the urinal, you have to drop your pants, pull forward your jockeys and slip down the pad. Only then can you pee. It is a bit revealing, because most men don't pee in public in this manner. In fact, when you see this going on, ask the poor bastard how his surgery went. You will notice a lot of this and understand now that you know what is really going on.

Day 37—second check up. They want me to drink a lot of water before the exam. The reason is that I had to pee into a device that measures the pressure of my stream. It was good. They asked if I had had an erection yet. I thought that this was a really stupid question. Erections don't seem too important when you are wetting your pants.

Day 70—Making progress. I only pee in my pants when I get in and out of cars, sneeze, and, o.k. after I have three martinis; well three doubles.

Day 107—Another exam—PSA is 0, not measurable, I am cancer free. I am going to die from something else.

Day 109—still drip. Still no hard on.

Day 268—First 24 hours with no diaper. Throw them away. I kept one. Dr. Roehrborn told me that some men can't throw their pads out. They keep them because they aren't confident that they will never need them again. Do it, they are a crutch. You can Kegel through it.

It is time to rededicate yourself to Kegels. If you back off you might lose the muscle strength and you will be back to pads. Need motivation? Consider the alternative. I was talking to a friend at a local bar and the conversation got around to prostate cancer. I got him laughing about some of the issues and asked him about his commitment to Kegels, because he seemed to be somewhat of a Kegel slacker. He said that his only problem was when he golfed. I had learned that there is a product for these activities. I decided to check it out, just in case. In fact, Brad, the physician's assistant, had given me the info on them. It was advertised for "Active Lifestyle Male Incontinence Control." "UNIQUE SHAPE AND SIZE IS DISCREET AND EASY TO REMOVE." 10 Count—One size fits all." How can one size fit all? Maybe porn stars don't get prostate cancer.

Why not give it a try? They are expensive, but Brad told me that some insurance companies even pay for them. Mine did so I ordered some, nice to try all the options available. They came in the mail and I wondered if you wash them and reuse them after use. The answer is yes. You wash them out, but you do not hang them on the line to dry. They are a pouch made of plastic-like material. They are 4 inches long and 3 inches wide. So big that one size will fit all. A four inch diameter is even big enough to fit over the head of a porn star. There is a plastic squeeze collar on the top. You squeeze to open the pouch. You place it over your little head and it closes up. Holy shit; did that hurt. It felt like putting an industrial size paper clip over your small head and releasing the tension. I thought I was going to faint.

So, I offer this piece of advice again. Before you have prostate surgery, start a program of Kegel exercises. If you need motivation, do this. Go to Office Max and buy a giant industrial style paper clip capable of holding 70 pages tightly together. Take it home and put one over your little head and release it. I guarantee you will decide to become the Jack LaLanne of Kegels from then on.

Day 393—First golf. I am sure I could have played golf much earlier, but the truth is I hate golf. It takes too long and requires too much work to have fun. Entertainment should be, well, entertaining. I have a lot of friends who golf and my wife wanted to play couples golf, so I agreed to play nine holes.

If I have to play more than nine holes, I fixate on how many holes I have left to play. These finishing daydreams only hold for the last three holes when I play nine. I bring golf up, only because a common thread I have heard from "fellow prostators" is that the biggest incontinence issues are on the golf course. This drives them crazy. Because of these warnings, I was a bit concerned. This concern was heightened since I had thrown away all my pads, months ago. Also, I was wearing khaki shorts. I had no leakage. So if you are a golfer, you have more incentive to Kegel or hit fewer strokes. Practice strokes are out. I must admit that I did not drink during these nine holes. We teed off at 7:30 am and did not bring a cooler. Nor were there any cart girls selling drinks, so I guess it really was not a real test. For me golf usually is a drinking sport. I think that is true for most folks. In fact in Minnesota and Wisconsin, where I grew up, every sport is a drinking sport. I never met an ice fisherman who doesn't drink.

Day 415 and I will make this my last report on Kegels. My wife and I decided to go to New York City to see some plays. We were motivated by a review we saw in *The Wall Street Journal* of a redo of *Waiting for Godot* by Samuel Beckett. In 1966, I had been in a production of *Godot*. This production featured such well know actors as Nathan Lane and John Goodman. During the intermission of *Godot* and then *South Pacific* by Rodgers and Hammerstein the next day, I observed something that startled me. First the audience was old. It appeared that the average age of eighty percent of the audience was seventyish. This should mean good markets for theatre in the next 20 years, as Boomers turn 60, but it does not portend good things for the long term. Very few young people were attending. It may have had something to do with the shows we picked. I was startled to witness a mass exodus of men to the rest rooms at intermission. It appeared that all the men were going to pee, myself included. This is a change in behavior over the decades. In our 30s and 40s, the women would run off and pee. In our 60s and 70s, the men run off to pee. Given the size of the Boomer generation, businesses need to expand the number of urinals.

Day 475 and this time is really the last report on leaking. One night we were invited to meet some friends at a local watering hole. I was running late. I planned to wear jeans and mine were all in the dryer. I pulled out a pair and left the house. They were still damp in the seams. The rest of the evening I had bad memories of the pad period of my life. Never wear wet pants. It does not matter why they are wet. It is just a bad memory you do not need to trigger.

The next, and surely not less important issue, is impotence. I bring it up after incontinence, not because it is less important, but again it is hard for me to imagine being concerned about the high hard one, while pissing in one's pants. Even more to the point is how would women be interested if you are still wetting yourself. This is yet another reason to get going on the Kegels. Then you can get to the really important thing.

That would of course be "The High Hard One" as my friends used to say. Used to say are the operable words here. Maybe that is one of the primary reasons that Boomers are so unhappy with their sex lives. Many newspapers reported in large headlines in late 2010 that the "Boomers are not so satisfied with sex lives."They were reporting on a Associated Press—Life GoesStrong. com poll that showed that only 7% of people between 45 and 65 say they are extremely satisfied with their sex lives. 25% of Boomers say they are dissatisfied. These boomers are the same folks that pioneered the sexual revolution—that would be the first part of "sex, drugs, and rock and roll." I have talked to many fellow prostate veterans. I am sorry that I can't report much optimism here. There is of course the implant or injection option.

My wife's GP asked her about my progress with the impotence issue. When she told him about the suggested injections, he responded that the thought of injecting himself in his penis, I don't think MDs use the term "wieners," but I may be wrong—made him feel faint. Me too.

That first summer after surgery I went to a 4th of July party. I was the eighth man to sit at a picnic table with all men a bit older than I. One of the men, whose wife had talked to my wife earlier in the summer, asked how I was doing. This caused the others to inquire, "Doing from what?" I told them about my surgery. It turned out every one of the eight men at the table had experienced prostate cancer surgery. What's the probability of that? Dr. Roehrborn was surprised by this incidence when I told him. He was skeptical. I told him it was because they were all old Swedes or old Norwegians. I meant it as joke. He didn't get it and informed me that Scandinavians did not have that high an incidence of prostate issues. I should have remembered from my childhood not to joke with Germans.

The alpha dog of this group then went on to say he had injected himself because nothing else had worked or helped to return to a teenage erection. The problem for him was that he still had an erection three days later. He went to his MD. They airlifted him to the Mayo Clinic. To let the air out? Actually, it's your blood that has to be let out, but I like the idea of air better. The "problem" is called "priapism" and it is very painful. This frankness promoted quite a stir, with the general conclusion that no piece of ass was worth it. I didn't bring it up, but I think this general consensus of the group's reaction to this story needs at least one disclaimer. We could call it the Marilyn Monroe option.

As the summer went by, I saw many guys I had known for a long time. I was surprised at how many had been through prostate surgery and how many did not talk about it. We don't seem to be able to talk to other men about these sensitive issues. This piqued my curiosity, so on the next trip to my urologist I looked at the support group literature that was in the waiting room. Whoa; the pictures of the men in the group looked like my father and I'm 64 and I look 55 (ok, 59). I don't want to meet with father figures and talk about erections, or the lack thereof. As I remember, we Baby Boomers never talked to our fathers about sex. We had the great experience of learning about sex from our buddies recounting their Saturday night triumphs on Sunday, driving around and drinking beer, and of course, lying about our successes.

Out Damned Spot: Another C

Then, of course, there are also the impending skin cancers. "In the day," we played outside. Our parents were never concerned about our skin safety. We were never told to come in from the sun's dangerous rays. The world was not full of perverts. We and our parents were not worried about "funny" strangers, so when meals were over and we did not have to be in the house, we were outside with the neighbor kids. We had not been beaten up about the danger of the sun so we got plenty of it. We often got sunburned. By the time it was time to return to school we were leathery looking. After age 60, the skin cancers begin to appear; Basal Cell Carcinomas.

When I was in my 40s, and a dean at Clemson University, I met every Monday with a group that called itself "Tree House." They met in a garage loft. We had several drinks. We heard the same old sex jokes repeated. We vowed not to talk about health issues, and we played one hand of show down poker with $5 bets. The "winner" of the pot was responsible for bringing the following Monday's dinner.

These Monday night get-togethers were very enjoyable. The members had been doing this since they returned to Clemson, the town, from WWII. For some reason, they invited me, a young newcomer to town, and even more surprising, a Yankee, to join their group. You could have scripted the event. The 90-year-old General had his one cigarette of the week and always asked, "Can we talk about teen-age pussy?" The textile executive would always say, "Pussy, the worst I ever had was magnificent." You get the idea. In fact, the stories were so repetitive, the Tree House Members would hold up fingers behind their head and flash their finger indicating it was the 10th or 10,000th time they had heard this same story.

I often joked with them that we should also have a bet on the number of purple scars from healing cancer removals we would see week to week. Now it is happening to me. It appears to me as I look around, that this is not a major problem. It is more like a phase we all have to go through if we had lots of fun in the sun as kids. It is no big deal if you take care of them by going to your dermatologist and getting the liquid nitrogen treatment.

As your scout I can report that you will be amused at work about how many of your fellow aging Boomers have bandages on their faces. But be sure to go to your doctor when you spot them. It may be a humorous passage of aging, but if they are not treated properly they can metastasize and that is in no way funny.

5

Globaloney Part 1:
Global Warming and Economic Forces

Globaloney: 1. an ever expanding discussion of proposals and plans designed to "solve" global warming issues. These solutions require people to act in "the global interest" to prevent catastrophic outcomes which will occur after these same people are long dead. 2. A new religion that assumes technology is stagnant or irrelevant. 3. A new Luddite- like belief that if we stop modern progress we will be better-off. 4. A siren call for international government, sometimes using Marxist rhetoric. 5. Pure and simple horse shit.

Graduation speeches are usually full of a lot of pompous BS. Over the years I have been collecting quotes from them, and here are a few that are particularly bothersome to me. Fellow Boomers have been giving them in increasing numbers. This trend will continue as we Boomers are now the correct age to begin pontificating. *The Wall Street Journal* reported that many of the speech-a-fyin' Boomers have been apologizing for how we screwed up. In this age of global thinking and anti self interest, they touted this theme over and over. Their advice to the graduates was "don't be like us." An example was Indiana Governor Mitch Daniels (61 years old) who told Butler graduates that, "Boomers have been self-absorbed, self-indulgent, and all too often just plain selfish." Montana Governor Brian Schweitzer (54 years old) also told graduates that the Boomer generation was "plain selfish." Thomas Friedman (65 years old), sounded the same theme at Grinnell College, telling the graduates that Boomers were, "the grasshopper generation, eating through just about everything like hungry locusts." Before I read this, I liked Tom Friedman because I liked his book a great deal (*The World is Flat*, Farrar, Straus and Giroux, 2005), but this statement is foolish. It must have made my favorite Friedman of all time, Milton, spin in his grave. Milton Friedman taught us Boomer economists that self interest is a fact of human nature. Those who ignore it will have flawed analysis. It will cause them to make very bad decisions in business and in life. Now, it is not nice to dwell on self interest these days, but it is one of the cornerstones of economic analysis.

I don't know if these commencement speaking Boomers were stoned in college, but they surely must have cut their introductory economics course. Maybe they were part of the know nothing crowd that avoided economics because it was "too hard." Somehow they missed the concept of self-interested and maximizing behavior. Individuals maximize satisfaction and firms maximize profits. Adam Smith wrote about this basic point in 1776. He gave self-interested behavior by producers and consumers as the reasons and the causes of *The Wealth of Nations*. Hello, do-gooders. Self-interest is not new to Baby Boomers. If you think you can change these basic instincts, you will be disappointed and you will make incorrect assessments of how the world works. You can disparage these basic instincts if you want, but you can't change them. If you want meaningful change, you'd better figure out a way to channel self-interest in the desired manner. Asking anyone not to follow their own self-interest is not a solution to anything. It is preaching. Have you noted the religious fervor of Green missionaries? For some time, I was confused by the fact that many of my friends and acquaintances were angry with me when I expressed disbelief in many of their Green arguments. Then it came to me. My father always told me to avoid discussing religion and politics with people. Globaloney is both religion and politics all rolled up into one system of belief. Repent or rot in hell. Or keep quiet if you don't agree with me. I am sick of them and their self righteous new religion. And I can't be quiet.

The Science of Global Temps

Of all generations, we should be careful about this climate hysteria. After all, we lived through it once before. I hope you remember it, or maybe like the Beach Boys, you need to hire an historian to teach you the history you missed. In the event you missed it, it goes like this. Carl Sagan was a very famous astronomer and professor at Cornell University. In 1980, Sagan was an anti-nuclear activist who hosted a TV series called "Cosmos." Sagan recruited some other scientists, and as a group they claimed that nuclear tests were creating dust and debris that would block out the sun's rays. They went so far as to say that Europe would be thrust into a new ice age. Continued nuclear testing would create a nuclear winter. This was science used to promote a political agenda. Sagan appeared on Johnny Carson forty times. He promoted his theory as if he were selling soap, not presenting science to peers. As late as 1991, Sagan appeared on "Nightline" "and argued that the burning oil wells from the first Iraqi war would cause monsoons and alter the environment. Three days later, black rain fell on Iran showing that the environment was cleaning itself before the soot got into the atmosphere. This mostly ended the argument.

Sagan died in 1996. Since the fall of the old Commie USSR, and the opening of some Soviet files, there is evidence that this theory was planted by the Commie propaganda machine. There was hope that antinuclear activists in the West would pick it up and rally against the introduction of Pershing II missiles in Europe. This seems to me Déjà vu (all over again, again), famous scientist predicting doom for political reasons. The nuclear winter became a political movement. Al Gore, do you remember Sagan? Could global warming, like global cooling, also be a political movement, with real or manufactured "facts" for political gain? Vaclav Klaus thinks so. Vaclav Klaus knows a little about repression. He lived in Czechoslovakia under the Russian Boot and became president of the Czech Republic after the rotting away of the USSR. Klaus does not see al-Qaeda or Muslim extremism as the main threat to freedom in the twenty-first century. Instead, he sees the threat coming from the environmental movement.

"We succeeded in getting rid of communism, but along the way with others, we erroneously assumed that attempts to suppress freedom, and to centrally organize, mastermind, regulate, and control society and the economy were matters of the past, an almost-forgotten relic… The reason for my concern is the emergence of new and very popular isms. I see a problem in environmentalism as an ideology. Environmentalism only pretends to deal with environmental protection. Behind their people and nature-friendly demeanor, the adherents of environmentalism make ambitious attempts to radically reorganize and change the world human society, our behavior, and our values" (*Cato Letter*, Summer 2007).

Time will actually solve the scientific issue. We will either have global warming or we won't. The problem is that most of us will not be around to say, "I told you so." Hey, a la Sagan, it has been recently suggested by some scientists that the cheapest way to solve the global warming problem would be to create some type of dust in the outer atmosphere to block the sun's rays a little. Ironic isn't it?

We will likely find out that technology can solve this problem because do gooder action will not work. It will not work because some very strong and fundamental economic forces work to torpedo voluntary Green solutions. These forces are self-interest, the public goods nature of the environment, externalities and present value. They are as unrelenting as gravity. First, consider the public goods issue.

Global Greenism, Public Goods and the Free Rider Problem: A Tale of Two Free Riders

The real problem with the hysteria about doing something about global warming is that powerful economic forces work against doing something. These forces are to be found in the public good aspects of the environment. Economists define a public good as a good that is non-excludable and non-rivalrous in consumption. This is unlike a private good that is excludable and rival in consumption. That seems a bit like mumbo-jumbo, but it is really pretty simple and important. A martini is excludable. People can be prevented from consuming martinis, because someone owns them. That someone is the person who serves it to you in their home during cocktail hour or the person that sells it to you in a bar. A martini is also rivalrous in consumption. That is economist talk for the fact that it is used up in consumption because it is consumed. That is if you drink it, it reduces another person's ability to drink it. It's gone, consumed. Public goods are different. Take a poem or an anti-aircraft gun. Once it is produced you can't keep others from consuming it, and it isn't depleted by your consumption. It seems funny to say it, but it isn't consumed in consumption. Unlike the martini, it isn't gone. Highways, radio frequencies, and national parks are more examples. Public goods aren't depleted in consumption, but they can become congested. Perhaps a clearer way of saying this is that people cannot be prevented from using a public good. One person's use of it does not prevent anyone else from using it. Some people may not even want to consume it. In fact, in a public good, like an anti-aircraft gun, even pacifists have to consume it. This is true even if they hate the military. That all sounds pretty simple, but it gets complicated because people will try to "free ride" on the provision of the public good. In other words, they will try to avoid paying for it because they can still consume it free once it is produced. As a result of all this payment avoidance, the "optimal or correct" amount of the public good is not is produced. Public goods will be under produced. One solution is a group might form a private club or a governmental unit to produce the correct amount (for the collective them) of the desired good. Golf courses and police forces are good examples, as we have private and public versions supplying these same public goods.

Consider another example of this somewhat confusing, but critically import economic principle. Golf courses present an interesting example because of the redistributive nature of golf as a public good. It is possible to restrict people from consuming golf at private clubs. All you have to do is prevent non-club members from being on the course. There is really no good reason for golf courses to be publicly financed. I was reminded of this while watching the rain soaked 2009 US PGA Open at the Beth Page Black course in a state park in New York. The TV coverage used lots of filler because of the many rain delays. One often-repeated short touted that this magnificent course was a "Muni," meaning a municipal golf course, a course paid for by taxpayers and used (mostly) by rich folks. It was implied by the coverage that these Muni courses were a good thing for governments to do. There is an important point in this. All publicly provided goods are not public goods in the way economists use the term public goods. A public golf course, like a public ballet, is simply a transfer from all taxpayers to rich folks. This is because it is (mostly) higher income people who golf or go to ballets.

During the cold war with the Soviets, I was often amused by people who visited the USSR. I taught "Soviet" Economic Analysis so they always wanted to chat me up when they returned. I always told them the whole system was a fraud, even worse, a fraud run as a prison for the benefit of the party members. They sometimes argued with me. Many times I heard the refrain that they were impressed by the ballet, by the museums, and theatre. They even had ballet and theatre for children. "If only we could do some of those same things here for our children." Yes, but the Soviet children did not have food and many other things, like access to knowing what was going on in the world, even or in Moscow. Their parents did have lots of vodka. Most importantly, most of the children could not attend. The goodies Western visitors saw were reserved for the "Nomenklatura." The Nomenklatura was the system of bureaucratic privilege in the worker's paradise, only the workers weren't part of it. It isn't surprising that the worker's paradise had such a ruling class. What is surprising is that they were so successful in hoodwinking Western visitors about it. I tried to explain to students that the USSR was a shit hole place to live if you weren't a party member. But students mostly believed the commie propaganda. Except on my tests.

But, I digress, back to public goods as in public goods in economic theory, and how it complicates the global warming issue. A very critical part of the definition is that once it is produced you can't exclude people from consuming it. The provision of the public good can be done by local governments, as in schools, or by the federal government, as in national defense.

Take public schools as an example. It is a well-known fact that some school districts produce higher quality education and that attracts people with kids. People actually shop school districts when they move to larger cities with many different school districts. The housing prices in these competing public clubs then go up. People then can join school district "clubs" by moving there. They are actually choosing to pay for better schools in terms of higher taxes. As the housing prices go up, the residents can produce even better schools. Many liberals don't like local public education because they don't think it is fair to people who cannot afford the high priced housing. They propose Robin Hood tax programs to have state property taxes rather than local property taxes for education. I remember when Arizona approved the building of a nuclear plant to generate electricity. They put a state property tax on the plant because it was viewed as unfair for the local district to get all that property tax revenue. "They would have so much tax money the band uniforms could have had 24-carat gold buttons." They were forced to share the tax revenue, but not the risk of living near the power plant.

Free Riding is a term economists use to explain individuals' behavior in the presence of public goods. It is just like breathing. Most people will try to free ride on the provision of public goods. This free riding behavior holds in spades for Green stuff, like clean air. Let me give you a very real world example, so real world it actually happened. This example demonstrates how difficult the private provision of a public good is in the real world, even for a very local public good in a small community; or as economists might say a small club.

I live in community on a lake in North Central Minnesota. There's so much lake shore that it is named Lake Shore. For the sake of this story, let's call Lake Shore, a village. It is definitely not a global village. It is really a village, village. There is not much diversity in the village. People look alike and they talk alike. This group homogeneity usually makes the supplying of public goods easier, or as economists would say, more efficient, as in cheaper. It is more efficient because homogeneous, small groups voluntarily support each other to a greater degree than diverse groups. An example in our history is farm neighbors often rebuilding barns after a fire . Another good example in a much larger group would be supplying the public good redistribution in the Mormon community. Mormons are a very homogeneous group, and they voluntarily share more of their income than most other groups. It will be interesting to observe what happens to Mormon voluntary redistribution as they become more diverse.

A few years ago, we were told by the Minnesota Department of Natural Resources that we were going to have a serious infestation of Forest Tent Caterpillars in our birch and white pine trees. The two species are very desirable, and we like them. The dense white pine forests were the primary reason for the economic development of the area in the mid to late eighteenth century. We also have Jack Pines which are not as much appreciated.

Almost everyone in Lake Shore lives on either side of a 10-mile road. Here home values are much affected by which side of the road you live on. Tier 1 property is on the lake side of the road and owners have lake access. Tier 2 properties are across the road from the lake. This is the land of the blue eyed folk. But there is lake property and non lake property.

A local do-gooder, Chuck Stuck, came up with a great idea. I am not making this up; his name is really Chuck Stuck. I would like to go drinking with his parents; they must have had a great sense of humor. Chuck put a group together to provide for a local public good to fight the infestation. Each of the neighbors would contribute a pro-rata share by lot size and the money would pay for a helicopter to spray our yards and save the trees.

The other players in this mini-drama are Vince Anderson and the some other villagers. Vince Anderson, that is Anderson with an "o" not an "e." "O's" are Norwegians and "e's" are Swedes or maybe Danes. And it matters. At least it matters to them. I don't care. I guess that makes me politically correct in a N. European sense. In fact I might even have it wrong. "E's" may be Norwegians and "o's" may be Swedes. It is too hard for me to keep it straight. They all look alike to me. They even all have blue eyes. Vince is what the locals refer to as a "Jack Pine Savage." A Jack Pine savage is, in the parlance of the South, a Red Neck. Jack Pines, unlike White Pines, are small and gnarly; they are never going to amount to anything.

Rednecks and Jack Pine Savages are usually pretty easy to identify as they almost always have junked cars and other such stuff, piled in the yard. There is almost always more than one lawn mower sitting unused in their often large, half mowed yards. They also start a lot of projects that they never finish. That is why, while he has a funny act, I don't think Jeff Foxworthy is really a redneck. He is successful and finishes what he starts. I first ran into the southern version of Red Necks in rural Virginia. Nice people if they like you. Our neighbor in Virginia owned an excavation business. He put it this way: "A red neck can fix anything, but the results are always a big God damn mess."

Village, Village, Jack Pine Savage Lawn Decoration.

Vince is also a sometimes-environmentalist. He has been known to turn off the ignitions of idling cars in town in the winter. When it's -37 degrees, some folks let their cars run when they shop. Along this line, a politician in Texas advocated a bill that truckers could not idle their engines when delivering goods or when parked in a truck stop. Hey, man, it gets over 100 degrees in Texas. Vince's sister, who lives down (or is it up?) the road, has a gigantic lighted Christmas display that I'm sure can be seen from outer space. I like this display as it tells me it is "the season." Even if I didn't like it, I would view it as none of my business. It is her land and her electricity bill. There is even a public good, or more correctly, a public bad example here. Some communities pass deed restrictions that prohibit some public goods. In some communities in Arizona, they have deed covenants that disallow stone or gravel yards, requiring that you plant grass. Or at least they used to; that is now (probably) very politically incorrect. Think of the water it wastes. Think how value laden and judgmental the word "wastes" is. Waste is not a word found in libertarian dictionaries.

Vince washes and dries his clothes outside, but not at -40 degrees. He also buries stuff, like batteries, oil, garbage, and other stuff. He refers to his private landfills on his property as his "nests." The next owners better get an environmental audit before they buy. As I said before, Vince is a sometimes-environmentalist. He thinks others should protect the environment for him. He is what in the public goods literature is called a free rider. Vince claims to likes Green stuff, but he does not want to pay for it with his private actions or money. He wants others to pay for it. He is a classic free rider.

Back, to Chuck. Chuck canvassed the neighborhood and asked folks to help pay for getting rid of the Forest Tent Caterpillars. Almost everyone jumped on board, being grateful for Chuck's local organizing. Often the private supply of public goods fails because the organizing costs are too high. Almost everyone participated, but I really can't be sure because most free riders don't make it known they are free riding. I know Vince was a free rider because he was proud of it and told me. Vince was savvy. He knew in his bones that they could not effectively spray my yard and the neighborhood without spraying his yard that is part of the infected area. Effective eradication requires spraying the whole area. He could opt out of the payment and still consume the local public good. He could free ride on the provision of the good because it is non-rival in consumption and not excludable, once it is produced. Think about it for a moment. If people free ride in this village-village, how many more are going to free ride in the global village. Almost everyone I know will. I will for sure.

This demonstrates the mammothly (pun intended) difficult, if not impossible problem of dealing with global warming. Providing public goods is very difficult at the local level. It will be impossible at the global level. People will never even know who is free riding. You couldn't even holler at them if you knew because they speak a different language. Besides, I really don't care about future Japanese generations. As I said earlier, I am still pissed off about the Baton Death March and the Rape of Nan King.

The global do-gooders understand some of this. That is why they are concentrating on the young and making it a religion. But, this will not work because it is easy to fake Greenism and for that matter, Religion. Vince is a case in point. He plays like he is an environmentalist, but he acts like an earth scorcher.

Recently I experienced another very small village pollution problem. When I am in Texas, I live in a downtown Fort Worth apartment building. It is only ten floors with seven apartments per floor. This certainly qualifies as a small village with just seven family units per floor. It is filled with socially conscious, friendly folks. We mostly like each other. One weekend our trash closet on my floor was inadvertently locked. In the early morning I took out my garbage and could not open the trash room door. I, the environmental heretic, took the elevator up one floor to deposit my stuff in the appropriate can in my neighboring village. When I returned home later in the day my environmentally conscious neighbor had not incurred the slightest cost of going up or down a floor; she just dropped her garbage on the carpeting in the hall. Liquids drained out of the garbage bags staining the relatively new carpeting. So much for small village interconnected utility functions. That is economics jargon for saying neighbors in even very small villages don't really don't give a shit, even about their own environment. Speaking of shit, our village is a dog friendly village. I went to the first floor to get my mail. A big dog had pooped right in front of the mail slots. The "mother" of the dog did not bother to clean it up. I did. I have heard Kay talking to her little girl about the environment. But she does not walk the talk, even if it is just a one floor elevator "ride" away or her dog. I reported this to our manager and she told me that she would determine who the pooper was. I knew that was coming— hidden cameras to check on dog behavior. We will be next. Assume you are being filmed when you are recycling to make sure you are getting your shit in the right place.

Let's go to the other end of the spectrum. Vince is a village player. Let's see how a world player acts. Albert Gore, Jr. is a world player, no doubt about it. Winning a Nobel Peace Prize and an Academy Award are definitely environmental world player bona fides.

Albert Gore, Jr. is an American prince, or at least as close to a prince as we have in the US. Gore is Vince Anderson on the worldwide stage. He preaches a public goods approach to solving the problems, but he does not practice them himself. This should not surprise us. He, like everyone, faces incentives to be a free rider. Everyone does! He is only following his own self interest.

Tiny Village Pollution.

Albert Gore, Jr. was elected to the US Congress in 1976 and to the US Senate in 1985. He was born in 1948, making him one of our tribe. He is a Boomer. In 1992, he was elected Vice President with President Bill Clinton, also a Boomer. But he was no stranger to DC. He grew up in Washington in a hotel. You see, his father, Albert Arnold Gore, Sr. was also a US Congressman and Senator from Tennessee. Prince Al's mother, Pauline LaFon Gore, was the first woman to graduate from Vanderbilt University's Law School.

Since his father "worked" in Washington, he grew up in DC. He lived in the Fairfax Hotel and attended the prestigious St. Albans School and then went to Harvard, the only place he applied. Princes everywhere get to go to college where they choose. Now, his life was not all fun and games. His father made him do fifty pushups daily because he did not want his son to be a Capitol Hill brat. He also had chores to do on the family farm in Carthage, Tennessee. In fact, his bio states that he "toiled" on the farm in the summer. He served a requisite stint in the military.

He has rarely been held accountable for what he says and does. He claimed he invented the internet. His defenders, princes usually have "defenders," claim he never said he invented the internet and in some sense they are correct. What he actually said to Wolf Blitzer on the CNN program, "Late Edition," on March 9, 1999, was, "During my service in the US Senate, I took the initiative in creating the internet." Like all politicians he actually thinks government does things like create the internet. He is also reported to have claimed that he and Tipper were the inspiration for Love Story by Erich Segal. Al did know Segal at Harvard. But it appears to me that his claiming to be the inspiration for *Love Story*, would be a lot like me claiming that Harrison Ford based his portrayal of Indiana Jones on my performance of the Postman in *Come Back Little Sheba* at Ripon College in 1963.

You find Indiana Jones, I am the Postman.

Suffice it to say that Al Gore is an environmentalist. He has that Academy Award and a Nobel Peace Prize to prove it. He also believes that we are in deep shit, environmentally speaking. "Two thousand scientists, in a hundred countries, engaged in the most elaborate, well-organized collaboration in the history of mankind, have produced long since a consensus that we face a string of terrible catastrophes unless we act to prepare ourselves and deal with the underlying causes of global warming" (Speech at the National Sierra Club Convention, September 9, 2005). That is an exact quote—it seemed wrong to me so I checked it several times. But give Al a break; it's a speech, not an essay. Make no mistake about it. Al Gore is a SERIOUS environmentalist.

As "old" people used to say when we were kids, actions speak louder than words. In his 2007 Nobel Peace Prize speech, he ended with the phrase, "and we will act." Let's look @ how he acts. I use @ out of respect because he created the internet. In early 2007, the day after Al Gore's film, "An Inconvenient Truth," won an Academy Award, Drew Johnson, president of the Tennessee Center for Policy Research, claimed that Gore "is a hypocrite and a fraud when it comes to his commitment to the environment, judging by his home energy consumption." After this charge, Gore scurried to make Green changes to make his home more energy efficient. He added solar panels, installed a geothermal system, replaced all incandescent light bulbs with the efficient twisty ones, and overhauled the windows and ductwork. The Tennessee Center checked back after the work and found that his energy consumption went up 1,638 kwh per month, making his monthly usage 17,768 kwh per month. Average home consumption in the US is 11,040 kwh per year. This means Al Gore uses more than 19 times the energy in his Tennessee home than is used in the average US home. Even when I was a kid, I resented the "do, as I say rather than what I do" mentality. But, I did not know any princes, but there were none in Medford, Wisconsin.

Rotten Green Apple

Now, to an example of Gore's business relationships, he joined the Board of Directors of Apple Computers in 2003. Do you think he was invited to join Apple's Board because he created the internet? Of course not, VPs get these sort of "gigs." The Board has refused to release information on its sustainability strategy and its total carbon footprint (xceptionmag.com, January 29, 2009). A carbon footprint is an attempt to quantify the amount of damage a company, a person, or an activity is doing to the environment. When Apple's refusal to be forthright was made public, many serious environmental activists thought Al Gore should resign from Apple's board. But if he did, how would he afford those huge power bills at his enormous carbon footprint home and private jets?

Now Al Gore is not an evil person. He, like all of us, is following his own self-interest and free riding. But, if Al Gore is free-riding when he is so out in front on what he believes is the solution to the problem, isn't almost everyone going to free-ride? I think what is so galling to many people about Al Gore is the dichotomy between his public statements and his personal behavior. But keep in mind, it is just simple economics.

The lesson from both the American Prince and the Jack Pine Savage is a simple one. Everyone follows their own self-interest and, in the case of public goods, self-interest means free riding. In the case of global public goods, we will experience extreme free riding—whatever that is. Look, I paid Chuck Stuck for worm eradication, but I am not going to pay for cleaner air for Iranians in the year 2040.

I presented this free-rider argument to my MBA economics class last semester and one student actually got angry with me. After all, she was on the University Green Committee and had started a battery collection box in the hall. Some friendly readers have suggested that I am too mean to Al Gore. I don't think so, I would do exactly what he is doing, most of us would, but most of us would be discreet about it! Al Gore is doing what we all do, but it is difficult to be discrete when you are a former Vice President. I am sure his neighbors have similar energy consumption, but theirs is not newsworthy. Theirs is just normal.

Externalities

An economic discussion that is a close cousin to the public goods argument is the externality issue. In the production of almost everything, there are externalities. These are resources that are used in the manufacturing process that aren't paid for because they are free. An example would be in the production of steel. When we make steel we use clean air, just like we use other factors of production such as electricity, land, and labor. We foul the air, and the price of steel does not reflect the use of this clean air resource. In addition to negative externalities, there could be positive externalities. When you drive by a doughnut factory you smell doughnuts and if you like the smell of doughnuts you feel good. The doughnut factory did not charge you for the good feeling from the smell. Now consider local externalities—every externality is a local externality some place.

Back to my village-village, for one more example. Every 4th of July and even at other times, we have neighbors who shoot-off extensive fireworks' displays. Now, not everyone likes fireworks. I personally hate them. I am a patriotic American, a veteran, but I hate fireworks. My father-in-law who served in WWII hated them even more than I do. I have many neighbors who agree with me; most of them have dogs. Dogs really hate fireworks. Dogs should rule. My dog, Emma Mae comes down hard on the hate side. One of my neighbors is referred to by these fireworks haters as Mr. Firecracker. I don't know what the dogs call him. Mr. Firecracker is a serial fireworks display guy. He thinks the 4th of July is more than a weeklong event and everyone should enjoy his way of celebrating this week long event.

Now it's important to mention that making noise after 10 pm is illegal in our village. I am dropping the village, village, you get the idea, it is the opposite of the global village. In case you didn't know, shooting off fireworks makes a lot of noise. It is also illegal in the state of Minnesota for unlicensed individuals to shoot off, or even possess, rocket-type fireworks. These include the big colorful ones that whistle. Mr. Firecracker breaks both of these laws. I have called the cops, but not much happens. I am viewed as a flake, maybe even an unpatriotic flake, for sure a curmudgeon. He also gives me the finger when he drives his boat by my dock. My wife and I left our home this year because of the excessive noise. Think of that. We will leave our home because of a neighbor's illegal, disagreeable behavior. I raise this issue because it is a bit different than the public goods argument, but it works in the same way and underscores the fact that if people don't care about how other people in their village feel, how can you think they are going to give much thought to the global village. In fact, the whole idea of a Global Village is pretty foolish. Hell, people are often not nice to their relatives—how on earth do you think they are going to care about someone in—you pick the place, a faraway place in let's say 200 years.

I find fireworks an interesting topic in some other dimensions. The week before the 4th, it was reported on the "Today Show" that some communities decided to forego the fireworks shows this year for budgetary reasons. They then interviewed a woman who actually said on TV (you could not make this up) that she was extremely upset because "how else could you teach your children patriotism." How about visiting the nearest veterans' cemetery?

Also, on the fifth of July this year, the local Minneapolis St. Paul/ NBC affiliate reported a pollution alert because of weather conditions and the previous night's fireworks displays. Maybe, if you are a patriotic, global warming parent, you can't use fireworks to teach patriotism. And maybe if you are an environmentalist, you have to be opposed to fireworks.

This brings me to the second killer economic principle that relates to the atmosphere and global warming. That is the problem of present costs, future benefits.

Present Costs, Future Benefits

An essential tool in economics, finance, and business is the concept of present value. In 1982, when the *One Minute Manager* (Blanchard: Morrow) first came out, I was Dean of the Business School and Textile School at Clemson University. In that capacity, I had a great deal of interaction with South Carolina business leaders. One night at a dinner after a Textile Association meeting, we were talking about Blanchard's book. I joked that we should write a book entitled, "The One Minute MBA." This elicited a spirited discussion that ended with a paraphrase of the old real estate adage about location. One of the attendees offered that we could call it, "The Five Second MBA." It would have one page and six words: Present Value, Present Value, Present Value.

Present Value is a simple concept. Any business or economic decision affects costs and benefits or revenues over periods of time. The decision maker needs a way of comparing costs and benefits in different time periods. A dollar cost or a dollar benefit now is not the same as a dollar cost or benefit next year, or in ten years, or in a hundred years.

To compare future dollars (costs or benefits) for different periods with present dollars, decision makers calculate the present value of these future dollar costs and the present value of dollar benefits. Present value is "capitalized value" of the cost or the benefit. It is a future value discounted to the present. "Doing the numbers" is accomplished by "discounting" these future values. Babe Ruth was once asked by a reporter how he could justify the fact that he earned more than President Hoover. His reply was, "I had a better year than he did." And he did. A more important point in discussions about athletes' salaries is that many times the payments are deferred over years into the future and a million dollars in six years is not the same thing as a million dollars today. In fact, a million in six years at an 8% discount rate has a present value of $630,000. At 8% and twenty years, it has a present value of $425,000. At 8% and fifty years it is only worth $213,000. Most people today have some understanding of this, from lottery prizes, as they are a stream of payments. If the winner decides to take all the cash now, the prize is greatly reduced because of present value considerations and of course taxes.

Think about spending money now on the environment to receive benefits in the distant future. The numbers just do not work. If we are going to overcome these incentives, perhaps we need government to get into the act. Not. Of course that is what do gooders want to do. Remember, that is what has Vaclav Klaus so concerned. Even Pope Benedict has jumped into this world government discussion. In a new encyclical, he called for a radical rethinking of the global economy. He stated that we needed a "world political authority" to oversee the world economy and work for the "common good." Father, forgive him; he knows not what he says. The Pope doesn't worry me too much on this, or for that matter on any issue. It appears to me that even most Catholics don't pay much attention to what he says. It must be frustrating for him.

Maybe we should consider turning the environment protecting job over to those stealing bastards at the UN. They did such a great job of running the "oil for food" program for the common good of starving Iraqis. Who can we find to run the world for Pope Benedict's common good? Can non-Catholics apply? My opinion is that he should pay more attention to his priests' sexual behavior and let someone else run the world. But, as you know, I was raised a Lutheran.

6

Globaloney Part 2: A Modest Proposal for Preventing the Children of the World from Doom

This is not about eating children. It is not that sick. I just want you to think about their cute little carbon footprints.

I am a firm believer in technology and smart people. That is why I am so skeptical of the Globaloney rhetoric of the warming folks. But, for a minute, let's plan a solution. Pollution and emissions are positively correlated to population growth. As the world population grows, there is more pollution. Why should the rich be able to buy carbon credits? The burden of sharing the costs will not be evenly shared. Most people have ignored the distributional impacts of being Green. In truth, the price of most products will go up. All carbon credits aside, the poor will pay the greatest burden as a percent of their income in protecting the environment. Most Greenies shy away from discussions of the distributional aspects of the global warming debate. This is not surprising, as most Greenies are liberals and it probably bothers them because the poor are disproportionably affected by these costs. Even worse they behave like Al Gore.

My modest proposal is that if we are serious about the environment, we should establish a lifetime budget of pollution credits. A lifetime global footprint could be issued for every person when they are born. Along the way, at certain points in your life, you can sell parts of that budget as carbon credits to others; perhaps to people like Al Gore, who are consuming way more than their birth budget. Unless, of course, princes get a pass and receive unlimited birth carbon credits assigned to them at conception.

It could work something like this. If you never buy a car, at age sixty, you would get x number of carbon credits that you could sell. This has the secondary benefit of taking pressure off Social Security. A budget book could be created that would specify the different rewards for good global behavior and where to apply for your vouchers. These vouchers could even be backed by some agency of global government. The vouchers could be traded and these vouchers could evolve into a world currency. They could have a picture of the UN on one side and a polar bear on the other. The printing would declare the paper to be legal carbon tender and this would designate that it had to be accepted for payment of global legal debts. If you did not honor this currency, you could be hauled into world court. It might even say "In World Government We Trust" over the picture of the UN building on the backside.

Now you could earn these credits for all sorts of good behavior, in addition to not buying a car. When you bought twisty light bulbs, you could get a few. Planting trees would be good. It goes on and on. Reasonable people could agree on how to assign values to the desired behavior. In essence, we are already doing this. I Googled "carbon footprint" and found a site that allowed you to calculate the carbon footprint for your wedding. It included reasonable things like the number of people coming, how they were traveling, as by plane or car, and the distances. A couple could forego a wedding and get the carbon currency. They might even then use their carbon currency to make a down payment on a house. This is really a win–win–win proposition. It protects the environment, rewards the people sacrificing for the environment, and stimulates the housing industry. Talk about a shovel ready project.

I could go on and on with the menu of rewards for good behavior, but the people of the world will need a world agency to hammer these out, so I will not waste time here. Suffice it to say, it is a very do-able project.

Before we move on, permit me to speculate on the ultimate carbon credit. A major issue in the coming doom is our children, and their children. Get my drift? The ultimate carbon voucher might be related to the number of children one has. Let me provide two examples. My wife and I have no children. She is now post menopausal and I had a vasectomy when I was 25. In addition, remember I have had the big C. Our child birthing days are over and we have none. We apply to World Government Headquarters in Somalia. We are awarded with 100,000,000 carbon vouchers, which we can sell on carbon markets. This is a reward for the tiny footprint we have left, by not having children, grandchildren, great grandchildren, and great, great, grandchildren. It is barely visible. It disappears when we die. We could sell our vouchers and move to California, where housing prices will still not have recovered. Instead of being looked at with suspicion because we decided not to have children, we will be viewed as global humanitarians; maybe even Gandhi-like. This is a great change. Thirty years ago some folks thought we were selfish for not wanting children. In Arizona, where I taught economics in the 1970s at Arizona State University, our CPA argued with me that it was our duty to have children for the intelligence pool. We rejected that idea, telling him that it was an elitist argument. Whatever that means. How times have changed. Now we are global humanitarians. We are doing more to save the environment than anybody—save some Buddhist Monks in Tibet.

Let's go to the other end of the spectrum. If you watch the "Today Show," you have met the Duggar family. They are from Rogers, Arkansas. They have appeared on the "Today Show" after the birth of their last few children. Bob, the father, is 47 and Joshua, the first child, is 27. In December 2008, "Today" had them on the air from their home. During their spot, Bob held up a copy of their new book, *The Duggars: 20 and Counting*. I guess if you have 18 children, you better make every sale you can. I must admit to being troubled by making money off having a lot of children.

The Duggar website, duggarfamily.com, says, "Children are a heritage of the Lord." That gives me great peace, as it must mean God is not worried about global warming. He must know technology will save the day. If not, he would likely be way less generous with that heritage.

Consider the Duggar family footprint. Take an average person's lifetime carbon footprint. Call it X. That would make the current Duggar family carbon footprint 20X. But Joshua, the oldest son is 27. His father was likely 20 when Joshua was conceived. Then a kid a year was born. Let's assume that some of these kids say, 25%, will be so turned off by their experience that they won't have any kids of their own. Also assume that the other 75% will have some sense and only have nine kids; half of the parents' batting average. That means that in the next two decades they could produce 122 kids, 244 little carbon footprints. I would guess that would wipe the Duggar family carbon footprint budget out. They better move to Arkansas and live in a log cabin, oops; sorry they already live in Arkansas. All kidding aside, kids contribute a great deal to global warming. And these are just the grandkids of Michelle and Jim Bob. As they say, do the math. This is very big, and you might say exploding, out of control, footprint. It is only part of the story. In the year 2111, a Duggar could be elected governor of Arkansas on the basis of the family vote.

We get such mixed signals. A young woman with three rug rats in tow at Target lectures my wife because she asked to have some breakable bottles double plastic bagged. But Jim Bob and Michelle get celebrated on TV. Have we thought about these issues enough? One last, but notable example, is Octomom, Nadya Suleman; enough said. She already had 6 kids. I find it troubling that

Nadya views her womb as a clown car. Even worse, NBC put her on TV.

Both the Duggars and Suleman seem to have a regular gig on "Today." It seems to be a common denominator. Maybe NBC should have to pay for the carbon credits for both families. Maybe the Chicoms will get control of the world global warming organization and enforce a global one-child policy, as they have in the PRC.

Actually, Bill Clinton is a politician who has thought about the effect of fertility on the planet. Clinton has argued that a major solution to global warming is the empowerment of women. At *Fortune* magazine's "Green Conference," Clinton argued that, "In every society in which it (female empowerment) has occurred, putting girls in school, giving them access to capital markets, and labor markets, has happened, birth rates have declined" (*Fortune*, June 25, 2009).

The Politically Postured Face of Greenism

Much of the Green advertising that firms are putting forward is political in nature. It is the "we are doing our part" type of public relations. The other day, I was passing a Waste Management garbage truck that was spewing forth a brown liquid. When I passed the truck I saw a big green sign on the truck that said, "Waste Management: A Green Company." Now how in the world can a garbage hauler be a Green company? I have nothing against Waste Management. They do a great job of picking up our mess. But how can a garbage picker upper be Green? Come on—as we used to say when we were thirteen years old—if they're Green—I have a green ass-hole. No matter who you are or what you do, it pays to advertise yourself as being Green. This can be done because we have no definition of what constitutes a Green company, a Green university, a Green family, a carbon neutral footprint, etc. etc. etc. Hey. This makes free riding easier. You just have to proclaim yourself to be Green. The same holds for organic.

A recent Waste Management ad in *Smithsonian Magazine* claimed: "You might say it's our nature to do what's good for the environment." This is how Waste Management manages its Greenness. They burn trash to generate electricity. They claim, "the waste we collect helps power one million homes. Last year we recycled enough paper to save over 41 million trees; our landfills provide over 17,000 acres of wildlife habitat." They have figured out how to make a public relations issue an advantage. This is possible because we don't know what Green means. It is in the eye of the advertiser.

Finally, we don't really know if people and for that matter firms and governments are doing what they say they are doing. I once stopped to recycle wine bottles because I had many of them and I did not know what else to do with them. As I was dumping them, the "recycle" truck drove up. Simultaneously, I realized I had dumped the glass in the can bin. I waited for the driver to "confess" and asked him if I could help him separate the glass from the cans. He looked at me and grinned from ear to ear, while he told me; "don't worry—they all go in the same land-fill." Maybe you already knew that.

Green Stuff I Could Not Have Made Up: Bad Green Statistics

Universities are all in on the act, competing with each other to see who can be the Greenest. A large group of universities are weighing their enrollment-adjusted trash to see who can recycle the most. The University where I teach has recently removed all trays from the cafeterias to save on the hot water needed to wash them. I wonder if these projected savings considered things like washing the floors to clean up the spilled food. Maybe this one will have an unintended positive consequence in that overweight students might cut back as they only have two hands. The co-chair of the "President's Sustainability Program" reported that the program saved 98,000 gallons of water in September 2008. This made headlines. Later in the article the co-chair reported that the October 2008 water usage was 37,000 gallons higher than the previous October. The other co-chair added that this increase "may have been caused by additional events in the UC" (University Center). Wow! You would think universities would do better research. Wouldn't it follow that the September decrease could have been caused by fewer events in the UC? Most people would have controlled the data for the number of events. I guess not if you have a political agenda. I wonder if chairing the sustainability committee counts for tenure? My guess is that it insures tenure.

Green Grade Schools

Back to school and the Greening blather gets stronger. The do gooders recommend that you pack a waste free lunch for your kid. "Start with a reusable lunch box made from recycled material... Don't forget that you can reuse small plastic containers of the food you've already purchased. With this type of system, your kid will never have to visit the garbage can. Everything comes right back home." And then do you throw it away? "Bazura Bags of Canada sells lunch bags made from recycled juice boxes" (All from MSP *Star Tribune* October 10, 2010). Going back to school always seemed so much fun to me. But I don't think I could put up with the pressure today.

Green Majors

The *Chronicle of Higher Education*, a weekly newspaper "trade association" type magazine (June 8, 2009), reported that the National Disciplinary Associations in higher education have joined to form "The Associations Network for Sustainability." The twenty members include The American Psychological Association, The American Philosophical Association, and believe it or not, The American Academy of Religion (this makes the most sense to me). It gives their professor members something to believe in, since most of them don't believe in a god. This sustainability network is meant as a way for institutions of higher learning to play a leading role in developing and executing "climate neutral policies." Why not, if you can major in "Queer Studies" (their term) at Dartmouth, there certainly should be room for "Green Studies." My problem with cross-departmental studies is that there aren't many jobs out there for someone with a BA in Queer Studies or Green Studies for that matter. Maybe if you minor in accounting, the job outlook improves.

Now, maybe you, like me, don't care much about what goes on at Dartmouth. But get on the internet. There are "queer" programs in your backyard, supported by your tax dollars at public colleges and universities. I am not a bit homophobic so I must point out that there is a significant difference between acceptance and governmental subsidization.

Back to the "Green Studies Major." The description of the new association states, "A key goal of a liberal arts education in the twenty first century must be to equip graduates with a diversity of intellectual tools and learning experiences needed to insure the health of our planet with the help of supportive institutions and faculty members, they have the opportunity to construct a world and a culture that are vast improvements on the ones they inherit." Now I understand what is going on out there. I always thought that scientists and engineers were the last best hope of saving the globe. I stand corrected; scientists and engineers have been replaced by "do gooders" as the best hope for mankind. I take that back. Even though I have spent most of my adult life in University settings, I have no idea what they are saying. So much for higher education!

Almost every university has a Sustainability Director and an Office of Sustainability. Does this come at the expense of the math department and science professors? Of course it does. Another of those nagging economics lessons is opportunity cost. If you do something, you can't do something else. One of the reasons economists are unpopular is that they point out that the cost of any program is what has to be given up to have the program. Tuition and tax dollars can only be spent once. One newly appointed Director of Sustainability was quoted as saying, "I think the President's Sustainability Committee has done a wonderful job of getting the university started on the right track." We used to call this Brown Nosing. A university close to where I live recently promoted a new "Master of Science in Interdisciplinary Studies—Sustainability Track." This is what they claimed to be doing. "The program leading to the MS degree in Interdisciplinary Sustainability is designed to develop advanced sustainability analysis and evaluation skills that are necessary to implement and document sustainable initiatives within the changing marketplace. This program is ideal for individuals wishing to be change agents for their organizations and communities. The curriculum emphasizes the efficient and effective use of minimizing the impact on the physical and social environment." What? *Stop the World I Want to get Off*. I think the students should sue when they can't get a job. This may be why I had such a short tenure as a university president.

Currently on this same campus, groups are competing to see which group can recycle the "most," whatever that means, in a six week period. "We want everyone to recycle more so we can turn in our own weight." In what?

This is a serious undertaking; it is not like streaking. It is also not a local phenomenon. 567 schools are competing in the competition, labeled "Recycle Mania 2011." This is even an international competition. I wonder if students at the Indian Institute of Technology are participating in the competition.

What surprised me the most, maybe I should say "shocked me," but I won't, was a poster I found in the hall outside my classroom. The poster was advertising RecyleMania, "you can learn all about it on recyclemania.com." The poster was printed on very expensive cardboard that was not recycled!

I suppose we did things that made older folks shake their heads when we were in college, but I remember them as being fun, including beer and other mind altering refreshments, and I don't think we thought we were saving the planet. I vaguely remember it had something to do with war, and our lives. A bit closer to home than the planet.

Green Stuff I Could Not Have Made Up: Compact Fluorescent Light Bulbs

In the same category as the water saving toilet, we have the twisty light bulb. The water saving toilet was mandated by federal law and caused most people to flush twice, using more water. The compact fluorescent light bulb is a Green product to save electricity. It is much more expensive to begin with, and remember from your economics course, price is a function of the price of the resources used in production. So the carbon footprint of producing these Green light bulbs is bigger than the carbon footprint of producing the old ones.

But worse, the unintended consequences are well, plain scary. The Maine Department of Environmental Protection posted this warning on their website in 2008: "Don't vacuum broken bulb debris because a standard vacuum will spread mercury-containing dust throughout the area and contaminate the vacuum. Ventilate the area and reduce the temperature. Wear protective equipment like goggles, coveralls, and a dust mask, in essence a HAZMAT suit. Collect the material in an airtight container. Pat the area with the sticky side of tape. Wipe with a damp cloth. Finally check with local authorities to see where hazardous waste may be properly disposed." I was still worried about lead in paint, but you have to chew that. Our government is mandating peanut standards in schools to keep children safe when only a few students are at risk, and they are mandating mercury light bulbs for schools, which puts all children at risk. I would like to see that cost-benefit analysis. In the summer of 2011, some members of Congress tried to overturn the impending ban on "regular" bulbs, but they failed.

Flat Taxes on Flatulence

"Belching bovines and gaseous hogs may be helping to blast a hole in the ozone and the EPA is considering taxes on farmers" (Fort Worth, *Star Telegram* January 29, 2009). The EPA denies it, but the American Farm Bureau stands by the report. The EPA does report that cows are responsible for twenty percent of US methane emissions. The farm communities of course, think this stinks. The American Farm Bureau reports that this tax could amount to $175 per dairy cow and $87.50 per beef cow. It appears that dairy cows have more gas to burp than beef cows. The head vet at the Fort Worth Stock Show expressed the opinion that tax collectors would have a "helluva time trying to get numbers on beef cattle." That makes sense. Dairy cows would be easier to count as they have a "house" they return to each night. Beef cows are homeless. Maybe ACORN could count homeless beef cattle, and even register them to vote. They almost always have names. ACORN could then bring in their absentee ballots to be counted.

"Where can we dump this killer dust?" "Flush it, but flush it three times."

Cleaner Air Prolongs Life

Researchers from Harvard and Brigham Young reported in the *New England Journal of Medicine* (January, 2009) that between 1978 and 2001, Americans' life span increased almost three years to 77 and as much as 4.8 months of this was attributed to cleaner air. This really confuses me. Before this report I had almost been convinced by the Greenies that the air was getting dirtier. I suspect we will soon have a new government agency to reconcile these conflicting claims.

Please Don't Change the Sheets

On a recent road trip my wife and I stayed at a Holiday Inn in Kansas City. In the bathroom, I discovered an interesting door hanger. It said, "Along with many hotels across the nation, we believe it is our responsibility to minimize our impact on the environment. Therefore, it is our policy to launder guest linens every three days for those guests staying multiple nights. If you would like your linens changed more frequently, please hang this notice on the doorknob on the outside of your guest room door. We appreciate your support of this program." Is hanging it on the door meant to put peer pressure on you? Do you get reported to the Green Police if you want fresh linens? This is really a self serving cost saving program for Holiday Inn. I, for one, like clean sheets every day when I travel. That is one of the (few) nice things about business travel.

Green Dilemma

Wind energy turbines are loved by some Greenies. I think they are pretty. They move in harmony, like a poor man's ballet. The problem is that people who live near these turbines claim that they make noise that in turn affects their health. Even worse for some Greenies is that they thought wind power was an answer to some pollution issues. Now they know that that they also kill birds. One wind farm near Altamont Pass, California has killed about 130,000 birds in its lifetime. And these are not just crows. Between 75 and 116 golden eagles are sliced to death every year (*Forbes*, June 16, 2008). I think I will have a breakdown.

Let's Have a Green Cheer

The University of Wisconsin designated its 2008 homecoming game against the University of Illinois, a carbon neutral homecoming game. What does this mean? This is Madison. Is outdoor hurling carbon neutral?

Déjà Vu All Over Again

Pravda has reported that the world is on the brink of another Ice Age. "Many sources of data which provide our knowledge base of long-term climate change indicate that the warm twelve thousand year-long Holocene period will soon be coming to an end, and then the earth will return to ice age conditions for the next 100,000 years... Because release of CO_2 by the warming oceans lags behind the changes in the earth's temperature, we should expect to see global CO_2 levels continue to rise for another eight hundred years after the end of the earth's current interglacial warm period. We should already be eight hundred years into the coming Ice Age before global CO_2 levels begin to drop in response to the increased chilling of the world's oceans." Maybe Carl Sagan was on to something.

Fouling Your Own Nest

Twenty percent of all Americans admit to peeing in their own swimming pool (CBS *Sunday Morning* June 12, 2009). What percent will pee in the global pool?

Trash Police

Garbage collectors would inspect San Francisco resident's trash to make sure pizza crusts aren't mixed with chip bags or wine bottles under a proposal by Mayor Gavin Newsome. They could face $1,000 fines. From 1994 to 2000 my wife and I lived in Crested Butte, Colorado, ground zero in the left/liberal correct, think world. We would get bright yellow notes in our trash "reminding us" that we had not removed the plastic top collar of the tonic bottles. Also— they would not take rest of the container. The bright yellow scolding letter was the trash Nazi's scarlet letter. I always wondered who they thought they worked for.

You Are What You Drive

I always check out the drivers of eco-friendly cars with bullying eco-friendly bumper stickers. "You can't say I drive a Prius because it gets great gas mileage." No. If you drive a Prius you've joined a cult.

Even worse it turns out the Prius is unsafe, but I knew that in my bones. I could tell by looking at it. It doesn't even sound like a car. It is really unsafe, so unsafe the CEO of Toyota had to apologize on TV. And remember they have not apologized for the Rape of Nanking."

Other carmakers are racing to develop really small, really Green, non-car cars. One example is PUMA for Personal Urban Mobility & Accessibility. Oh, Oh. The Insurance Institute for Highway Safety recently concluded and reported that damage to micro cars in low speeds, like in three to six mph, could be expensive to repair. The worst was the Kia Rio that racked up a $3,701 repair bill in a six mph test crash. I wonder how the dummy fared. I wonder how many carbon credits that cost. My wife says I am not a good driver. I think I will keep my oversized pickup. It will make her happy, as she will know I will be safer.

Black Market Soap

Residents of Spokane County, Washington, are smuggling Cascade and Electra Sol Dishwasher Soap into town. Just pop over to Wallace, Idaho, visit the whorehouse museums, and buy some soap to smuggle home. I find this particularly amusing because I know some folks who used to buy dope in Spokane and take it to Wallace. This is a time dimension cross haul if there ever was one.

Why are they smuggling? Spokane County passed the strictest law on dishwasher soap with phosphates. These restrictions rarely work because states have pretty porous borders. I know this first hand because in the 1960s, Wisconsin had a ban on colored yellow oleomargarine, not black, not margarine for blacks. Yellow margarine. The dairy lobby was powerful. My father had psoriases and was advised by his MD not to eat butter. White margarine simply didn't taste right because it looked wrong. So whenever we went to Minnesota or Illinois we had to smuggle colored oleo into Wisconsin. You could, of course, color it yourself with yellow coloring capsules, but you can imagine what a "big god damn mess" that made.

State and local leaders have never learned the simple lesson of federalism and competing jurisdictions. Like the local public goods argument of schools and people moving to certain school districts, Americans can vote with their feet. If city or state governments pass high tax rates or do not solve local problems, people will vote with their feet. Rudy Giuliani understood this when he was Mayor of New York City. The Terminator did not understand it in California. On one of my stints in Washington DC, I lived in Reston, Virginia and worked at the Treasury Department. This was the early 1970s and Virginia had state liquor stores, with high prices, and all the charm of the US Post Office. Almost everyone would buy their liquor in DC and tote it home, even on the bus. There are many examples of cities, states, or even countries where the politicians don't realize that the ultimate impact of their excessively foolish behavior will be smuggling. If it gets bad enough, migration is another option. P. J. O'Rourke (*Driving Like Crazy,* 2009) pointed out that politicians prefer trains to automobiles, not only because automobiles permit people to freely move about, but also to move out of their jurisdictions. Think of it as the turnstile theory of government protest. If things get bad enough, you move to a different city (like out of Detroit), a different state, or even a different country. Very few people have ever moved out of the US, but many are moving out of California. About the only time folks have moved out of the US was when some of our Boomer brothers moved to Canada to avoid the draft during Vietnam. Some of them stayed. Different taxes and regulation is a major benefit of federalism. But state legislators never learn. They constantly raise taxes and the people escape to places like Texas, Arizona, and Florida—so they raise taxes even more. This only speeds up the migration. If you look at state tax rates and correlate them with state income growth, you will see the economic impact of people and business leaders voting with their feet.

Good Things Now Bad

Reusable shopping bags can breed bacteria. A study funded by the Canadian Plastics Association found that reusable shopping bags pose a significant food safety risk. It seems they are hotter and increase the cross-contamination of food, particularly if you reuse the reusable bags. You could clean them but they are difficult to dry. It's even worse if you put your jock strap in the same bag.

Tips on Saving Money on gas on your vacation reported on "The Today Show":

Don't pull a heavy object
Don't pack on the roof
Change your tire pressure when the number of people in the car changes
Know where you are going
You can save one mile per gallon if you don't run your air conditioning

This is the type of advice that makes "The Today Show" riveting, must viewing.

Green Things and Marriage Counseling

Some marriages are in trouble because even if one spouse is Green the other may be Greener. Examples abound. A Green family defies the mother. She likes locally raised bacon, whole grain bread and raw milk. They sneak Chef Boyardee products. "You're kind of in a perpetual state of feeling like you're not measuring up." Because of her husband's convictions, they layer up clothes. Her kids complain they are cold and they live like the Amish. I call a big horse shit on that. Growing up, I lived near Amish folks. They did not live like this; they did not drive cars, but they were warm in the winter. I guarantee it.

I also laugh at the idea that you have to make people feel guilty to get them to buy locally grown food. Most people consume local produce because it simply tastes better. People I know who grew up in the Midwest and no longer live there nostalgically long for fresh tomatoes and corn in the summer because it tasted soooooo good. If local stuff doesn't taste better, don't buy it. The local food Nazis can go to hell.

The university that employees me has a one book program for freshman. The programs are pretty common these days as part of freshman orientation.

The freshman get together in smallish groups and discuss the book. The book they recently picked was *Deep Economy* (McKibben 2008). About half this book is spent advocating local food to help the environment. Maybe next year they could read *Atlas Shrugged*. There is no chance of this, liberal faculty run these programs. They have bought into these arguments hook, line, and politics. I often wonder where these local food loonies are going to buy locally grown sprouts at Arizona State University in the summer or the University of Minnesota in the winter.

Who is Going to Pay for All of This?

A lot of resources, a huge amount of resources, no, a shocking amount of resources are going to be spent on Green things. Just how many? Does anyone have any idea how many resources these are and where they are going to come from? Let's see if we can make any sense of any of this.

First, we should revisit the concept of carbon footprints mentioned earlier. A carbon footprint is a measure of a person's impact on the environment, particularly on how different activities impact climate change. It relates to the amount of greenhouse gases that personal activities produce—you pig. Your footprint is measured in units of tons (or kg) of carbon dioxide equivalent. You have a primary footprint and a secondary footprint. Your primary carbon footprint is your direct emissions of CO_2 from fossil fuels including domestic energy consumption and transportation like cars and planes. It is often argued that you have direct control over these emissions. But, it seems to me the only times I have flown or driven and I had control over it, was a vacation. Since we take most vacations around business trips, the amount of such travel is very small. So I go back to when I was a kid. On these Sundays in 1953, our parents would load us in the car and we would ride around town. Cars were a pretty new luxury, and it was the family recreation. We drove around town, sometimes stopping to chat with their friends. The question of voluntary flying and driving is a difficult question. I think that only about five percent of my driving and flying is voluntary. Ninety five percent of it is to get somewhere I need to be to make a living or buy food.

Your secondary footprint is a measure of indirect CO_2 emissions for which you are responsible. This footprint is created by the manufacture and transportation of the goods and services you buy. The more you buy the bigger foot print you have. In other words, if you live in Wisconsin and have a glass of milk for breakfast, your foot print is smaller than your neighbor, that energy pig, who drinks coffee. The coffee transport creates more CO_2 than the milk delivery. It is pretty easy to find a carbon footprint calculator. Just Google "carbon footprint calculators" and you will find many for many different situations.

It is argued that it is a good thing to offset your bad environmental behavior by buying carbon credits. You could plant trees or purchase a case of twisty light bulbs. As you might expect, self-interested entrepreneurs have created markets that make this easier for you. You can buy credits from a firm that is planting trees to sell carbon offsets to people like you. Even firms that pollute can be Green Companies by purchasing these credits. Now I don't know about you, but this reminds me a little of the square inch of land I was given in Alaska for eating Shredded Wheat in the 1950s. If you think about it, this was a great promotion. Most kids don't have much innate desire for Shredded Wheat. But I ate my share, hoping I could put enough square inches together so I would have enough land to build a cabin. If I could find my deed I could sell them to Waste Management for their use of my carbon credits. Even better, if some of my square inches are in the Arctic National Wildlife Refuge (ANWAR), I am probably due some oil royalties.

You can find lists of many things you can do to reduce your foot size on the internet, things like turn off the light and air conditioning in your motel room when you leave the room. For short trips, walk. Think carefully about things you do in your spare time. This is giving me a headache. It sounds like my mother. Bingo, nanny state.

It is even possible to sell your carbon credits on eBay. Check it out. The idea is a simple one. If you pay me, I will do something to pollute less so you can pollute more—or pollute the same and feel good because you are Green. That is what Al Gore did after his bluff was called on his polluting mansion. He bought carbon credits. If you are rich it's easier to be Green.

So how much money can you make on eBay? There are guys who own Christmas tree farms who are selling the carbon credits every time they plant a tree. A couple of the big guys are making more money from the carbon offsets than they do from selling the trees. There is even third party certification of these carbon credits. The Chicago Climate Exchange is one. As I said before, you could not make these things up and I promise you, I am not making this up.

An important question is who is going to pay for saving the planet and what, are they willing to pay? The only attempt that I have seen is in a recent *Washington* Post/ABC News Poll. The poll found that Americans were willing to pay for protecting their children and grandchildren from global warming. The pollsters set up the question by explaining the cap-and-trade legislation in Congress. The poll results showed that 62% of those polled said they supported the idea that the government should regulate the greenhouse gases. The pollsters then asked if they would be willing to pay $10 a month more on the monthly electric bill to support the bill. Fifty six percent said they would; forty-two percent would not. Then they asked if they would be willing to pay $25 per month extra. Forty four percent said they would; those against rose to fifty six percent. Congress better listen up. A small majority of voters are all for the environment if it will only cost them $120/year, but not if it will cost them $300/year. As usual, politicians don't know much about demand curves. Nancy Pelosi probably thinks she can change them. If you think about it, the environmental movement often takes on the aura of a religious movement. That is because if you are going to change consumption patterns you need a religious fervor. The Boomers from the Midwest remember Friday Fish Frys were everywhere. Lutherans even went to them. When the Pope decided Catholics would not have to eat fish on Friday, they mostly disappeared. And even the Lutherans miss them.

7

Home Economics

When I entered high school in Medford, Wisconsin in 1959, there still were vocational subjects in the curriculum. So like every other freshman boy, I was required to take a year of either Manual Arts or Agriculture. The agriculture classes were mostly about dairy farming because we were a milk-producing area. The manual arts could be auto mechanics, metalworking, or woodworking. I picked woodworking, as I really did not want to get metal slivers in my fingers or grease on my hands. In woodworking class, I really only needed to be alert around saws to stay safe. The girls had to take home economics. I really would have preferred to take home economics as I liked to cook and bake even then, before they became an acceptable amateur manly pursuit. But boys couldn't take home economics. The more rigorous schooling that was motivated by the space race was just being integrated into the curriculum. Thank god we got out of the insanity of mandatory vocational education after only one year.

I think home economics, or perhaps it is more correct to say the economics of the home, should be an educational topic. Until one leaves home, home is the world. I find it difficult to teach economics to kids because kids don't live in the economy or the real world if you prefer. Many, even most, in the US don't face scarcity, and they usually don't have to make decisions between competing solutions. If these choices are considered at all, the decisions are made for them by the benevolent economic dictator in the household. In this sense, they live in a "command" economy albeit, a hopefully benevolent one. Unfortunately, I am sure some live with a Stalenesque dictator.

At some point in your life, maybe when thinking about dealing with your grandchildren, you should think about the economics of the world they inhabit or will inhabit. Maybe you even have young children from your second or even third wife from the Millennial Generation. These relationships are sometimes hard to describe. Would your son from your first marriage and your son from your third marriage be half-brothers thrice removed? Millennials are sometimes called Generation X, or even Echo Boomers. They are now turning 34 and still fertile. So it is conceivable that you have some "new" children younger than your grandchildren. It is a confusing world we live in. But kids adapt. It strikes me that today they don't give a shit about who their second cousin or half brother is from their father's third wife. It is ordinary. Giada was recently assisted on "Every Day Italian" by her 20 year old aunt who was her grandfather's daughter.

For lack of a better term, I like to think of the world you create for your children and grandchildren as part of a subject I call the "new home economics." It is not about baking a cake—it is about creating incentives to produce better behavior.

Perhaps the most important incentive operating in this version of home economics is what economists call "moral hazard." Moral hazard and adverse selection are part of the same economic incentives. Moral hazard is the proposition that if you are insured against the bad effects of something, you will pursue more risky behavior because the potential costs are mitigated to some degree by the insurance. Let me give you a simple example about houses built on the coast.

Moral Hazard

When my wife and I were first married and I was a graduate student at the University of Virginia we would go with a group to the Outer Banks of North Carolina. The first visit was a revelation for me as I had never before seen the ocean. The composition of this group was a reflection of the late sixties. The graduate students were all men and our wives were all teachers. Schools needed teachers and there were no rules that they have "education" degrees. Most of us were not from Virginia and were married. The first female economics PhD student also arrived in 1967.

Our group of fellow students and wives would go to the Outer Banks for a week after the spring semester ended. This tradition started in the early summer after our wives had completed their first year of teaching in Virginia's newly integrated schools. There were interesting experiences for our wives to pass on to us at the end of each school day. Susan thought most of the problems with integration came not from the kids, not from the parents, but from the local teachers. The women in our group, these "wife/ teachers" were short-term teachers from day one and included many Yankees, teaching their first semester in newly integrated classrooms in the rural South. Susan worked for the first black principal in the county, Miss Spriggs. Susan spoke Minesooota English and was actually asked more than once: "Miss Amacher, actually more like more like, "Mizzzzzz Ammacurrree, what language you speak?" It surely was not Southern; it was "Lake Wobeggonese."

The cabins on the Outer Banks were really basic. They were raised off the ground on power line quality stilts. They were high enough off the ground that we parked our cars under them. The insides were basic linoleum floors, few very basic appliances, Formica countertops, and the standard green melmac plates. It struck me at the time that these were disposable houses. And they were. All along the eastern seaboard, people built disposable houses. Houses blew down every so often from hurricanes or, particularly on the Outer Banks, they fell down because the Banks just moved. Sometimes these events were part and parcel of the same weather event. People did not have insurance because it was too expensive. It made more economic sense to self-insure and rebuild another throwaway vacation house after it was destroyed by a storm.

Years after graduate school days, Susan and I returned for a nostalgic visit. The old haunts were all gone. They had been replaced with beach-side mansions. Why? Had technology produced more hurricane resistant homes, or had we discovered how to hurricane protect the coast? No, the US government got into the subsidized flood insurance business. And the houses destroyed in a hurricane counted, as water was the cause of a great deal of the damage. The people most at risk were the first to sign up. Economists call this "adverse selection." That means that those most at risk are the first to sign up. You might think that this makes for a mighty risky polluted pool of insurance customers, not likely to attract private insurers. You would be right. To correct this "market failure" the state and federal governments became the insurer of last resort. I put quotation marks around market failure because it is not a market failure. The insurance market was just reflecting greater risk just like in higher car insurance rates for teenage boys. It might instead be labeled political failure. Poof, we had governmentally subsidized flood insurance.

Smart folks, who could now get insurance, tore down their shacks and built insurable mansions. Surprise. The next hurricane was the largest hurricane in history, measured in dollar value of damage. The next hurricane will be even larger, not because the wind was stronger, but because the houses will be more valuable. In essence, government subsidized insurance creates a bigger loss, a worse hurricane. Worse as measured by how much damage they caused in dollar terms. This is what economists call moral hazard.

In August of 2005, Katrina hit the coast of Louisiana and Mississippi and we had one of the largest national disasters in US history, and we got to watch it on TV. Rescue efforts were widely criticized with the director of FEMA in the spotlight. There was plenty of blame to pass around, but most of it was directed at President Bush. This is to be expected, but I laughed out loud when I heard Michael Brown, FEMA Director, say we (government) need to work more like the private sector. Even business types don't get it when they go into government service. "Hey—Michael" the problem is that it is government. Period. It can't work more like the private sector because of the incentive "thing." The New Orleans problem included real criminals in the private sector, the corrupt politicians, and the police. Some of these police were even filmed looting. The biggest blame should go to those who insisted that we rebuild the city. Rebuilding the city just sets the stage for a bigger future disaster. Why not pay the claims, quickly and generously. Then announce that the federal government is saddened by the great loss and suffering, but is no longer going to fight Mother Nature. The FEMA Secretary could hold a news conference and announce: "The Dikes will not be rebuilt by the Corp of Engineers and publicly subsidized insurance will cease." What would be the result? First, the Mayor and other city officials would protest "this racist decision" and say they would go forward with their own plans to rebuild the city. Private insurers would not participate. Some entrepreneurial developers might propose a "New Orleans World" version of New Orleans three hundred miles or more north to insure it was out of hurricane harm's way. Most of the private business people and homeowners would take their insurance money and move away. Bingo—no future biggest natural disaster of all time to worry about. You see the essence of this is that government is subsidizing people to be in harm's way. I am not arguing that we should not help Katrina victims recover. I am only arguing that we should not tee-up New Orleans for the next big one. We should help them move to a safer place. Instead, the federal government spent $14 billion "repairing" the levees. I will bet you $14 or $14 billion they don't survive the next "really big one."

The same issue can be found in Florida. Florida has a state-run enterprise that insures against storm damages, "The Citizens Property Insurance Corporation." This has a nice ring to it. It sounds like an old Soviet style agency. The CPIC has an $18 billion unfunded liability. It provides below market insurance to Florida property owners in harm's way. To make things worse, the state of Florida also has a "Hurricane Catastrophe Fund" that regulates what private insurers can charge. So the private companies flee and you can't even buy private insurance if you are rich and want it. The state regulators admit that in high-risk areas, the insurance rates are as much as 35 percent below what is needed to cover potential claims. If you liked Katrina, stay tuned.

To complete this melodrama, in 2009, The Republican dominated legislature in Florida passed a bill allowing private insurers to sell hurricane insurance and charge whatever they wanted. At least three major insurers were interested. This would have been enough to have competitive pricing. The governor and future US Senate candidate, Governor Charlie Crist, portrayed this as a giveaway to big insurers, even though no one would be forced to buy this insurance. And he is a Republican—at least nominally. It was just another option. You know Crist; he was a McCain supporter and was considered a potential VP candidate. He is the one who looks like he spends six hours a day on the tennis court. Crist vetoed this legislation, with the result that now taxpayers can foot the bill for the next big one. And I thought Republicans were the ones that were market oriented.

How does moral hazard relate to my new home economics? It has the same principle. Your family is like an economy, and you are the government. Moral hazard in your home economy has the same economic force. If you fix up the results of risky or bad behavior, you are going to get more risky bad behavior. This is a very simple concept, but it is hard for some people to grasp.

A real world example might help. Many years ago, I was visiting an economist at UCLA, Armin Alchian. Professor Alchian was an economist I admired and I took him up on an invitation to stop to see him if I were in Los Angeles. Professor Alchian was nice to young economists and a ball buster to colleagues he thought were "wrong-headed." For a young economist, this is great fun and endearing.

We had lunch and after lunch we returned to his office. There was a student waiting to see him. He patiently asked what the student wanted. He soon realized that the student did not grasp the concept of moral hazard. The student could not see how government subsidized insurance protection against risky behavior, or even governmentally-mandated safety standards could influence an individual's behavior. Professor Alchian asked the student to consider a proposition and then answer a question. Instead of the car that the student had in the UCLA parking lot, with all the federally mandated safety features including seat belts, he was going to loan him an older car to drive home. It addition to not having seat belts, etc., this car was going to have an old timey knight's jousting pole welded to the front hood of the car with a sharpened end pointed at the driver's neck. He then asked the student which car he would drive home more carefully. BINGO, moral hazard.

Moral hazard is a critical part of my new home economics as it relates to bringing up children. If you, the family Czar, fixer-upper of last resort, fixes up all the problems that develop, you are going to witness more problems; be they drugs, impaired driving, pregnancies, bad grades, _____. You fill in the blank. If you make them go away with few consequences, if you insure against the costs, you will get more and bigger problems.

Does Moral Hazard Impact on Having or Not Having Children?

This is difficult for us Baby Boomers to grasp. We often behaved badly. But most of us didn't get caught and luckily skated through risky times in our lives. Another favorite economist of mine was Max Hartwell, an Oxford University economic historian, who taught at the University of Virginia on an irregular basis. Max once told me that he found it curious that so many couples in my age group were choosing not to have children. I told him I thought it was because the pill made it a choice. He did not accept this explanation, dismissing it by arguing that people always had a choice. He was a good economist and realized that the pill had just made the choice less costly.

The year after this discussion, Susan and I visited Max at Oxford. He was in charge of the University wine cellars so it turned out to be a very nice visit. Oxford University wine cellars are a great place to have discussions. He told us that he had been thinking about our earlier conversation about children and that he had even discussed it with sociology colleagues back home at Oxford. He claimed he had it figured out. He hypothesized that we were so shocked by both our own and our friends' risky behavior in the 1960s, that we viewed the costs of having children as too high and too risky, because of our own behavior. This of course is the fondly and probably exaggerated sex, drugs and roll experience. He said we understood that if our parents and the parents of our friends didn't have more influence on our collective behavior, how could we ever affect our children's behavior?

I have thought about this conversation over the years and related it to moral hazard. You don't discipline your best friends. Many Boomers with children have developed the concept of children as friends, even best friends. This is different from the Dr. Spock culture in which we were raised. We have gone from the Spockian concept of letting children be children to children as friends, even best friends, i.e., wanting to play with them. My gut feeling is that Boomers developed this children as friends culture, because they did not want to be grown up, i.e., parents. I must admit that I have difficulty with children as friends. I don't see how you can be the best friend with your child. You are an adult and they are children. I have even heard some parents say that the cops have "it out" for their kid, when the kid had clearly broken the law like driving 75 mph in a 35mph zone in front of our house. I remember saying the same thing when some of my friends got arrested for fake IDs. The cops really had it out, or is it in, for us. I always thought that if you want to be friends with a kid, you need to grow up. It didn't work very well for Michael Jackson.

We won't know if this new parental paradigm is good or bad for a couple decades. My thought is just that parents should wait until their kids grow up to become their friend. The young people I find interesting are those who had a chance to mature with a dependable role model. This is easy for me to say since I never had to be a dependable role model.

Think back to when we were kids. Our parents fixed things for us, but there were big costs to pay. If our parents did not fix them up, the county judge often fixed them up. In Taylor County where I grew up, the judge could be tough and he would almost always give the kid who screwed up the alternative of "jail time or joining the military." I was always surprised and impressed at how after a few years in the military with parents being replaced by a drill sergeant, the troublemakers returned as responsible veterans. It was such a sweet and enlightened solution.

I had a friend who is an accountant and he treats his children well. They know he is going to buy cars for them and pay for their college. He even helps them in graduate school. He understands the new Home Economics. He told his children he will always be there for them. However, they also know there are certain behaviors that he will not tolerate. A big one is tattoos. He told his kids that if they get a tattoo they are not going to be given anything, not one red cent, in his will. They believe him. This is a good threat. He is not saying that he is not going to be there if they need help. He is only saying he is cutting them out of the will. You could even use it as a grandparent. How can your kids think you are interfering with their child rearing, when all you are doing is talking about your will?

I hate tattoos. Tattoos are markers of really stupid behavior at one time in your life. Most bad behavior fades as time advances. Years later, some people even laugh about their past bad behavior. If you get Semper Fi tattooed on your forearm, you are likely to get a pass from most people, but you are not likely to become a corporate CEO. If you are an attractive female, a tasteful rose on your ankle may be okay. But, even in this case it is going to get saggy. My wife thinks the exception to this is a female Olympic athlete. In this case she argues that the five Olympic rings tattooed on her ankle will help her career. I agree with her on this exception. If you get tattoos down your arms and over your neck and torso, it is only ok if you are an NBA star. With these tattoos in the real world, you will never get a responsible job in the grown up world, unless you wear turtle necks and long-sleeved shirts every day and eschew company picnics. A good rule of thumb is that if you can't cover it with clothes, don't get it. This may not be fair; it's just the way it is. I recently learned that the kids of my tattoo hating former friend have boyfriends and girlfriends with tattoos. That is the kind of rebellion I find acceptable, as long as they don't get married.

Years ago I read an article about success in corporate America. The researchers defined "success" in organizations of all types and sizes. They then looked at pictures of the people they had defined as successful. It appeared to the authors that a very high predictor of success (measured by income) was looks, broadly defined, as tall, in shape, pleasant looking, well groomed, well dressed, etc. My conclusion is that if you have tats, you might consider trying to be an entrepreneur or go to work in the family business, if you have the luxury of being born into a successful one. Better yet, maybe Generation Ys will be successful in passing a law classifying people with tattoos as a minority. A minority of dumb shits. Each company, by then owned by the US government, could be forced to have a representative number of tattooed workers in their mix. The representative number would be the same as the tattooed folks in the population of work age. This determination could be part of the census.

It is interesting how many of the present generation of teenagers and early 20-somethings talk alike—"like," they talk in a monotone, from the back of their throat without making facial expressions, like, dude, I don't think we talk alike, do we? If we did, like, I think we outgrew it. I hope they can gain facial expressions as they get older or life is going to be boring when these monotones turn fifty. Maybe this lack of conversational voice comes from texting and emailing. They even text each other in the same room, rather than talking. Young adults are also doing it.

At a recent Packer game luxury box where we were guests, my wife was talking inside with a young man about his career goals. He was texting. She said, "I'm talking to you, you're texting, that's rude." He looked at her with that dumb look and since he was "raised right," he apologized and put it away. She then asked him ,"who are you texting?" He replied that he was texting his girlfriend. Then she asked where is she was? He pointed out side to a seat in the outer box. I wonder if this counts as foreplay.

Adults often think young people look strange. Think how we looked. Black leather jackets, DA haircuts, engineering boots. Early Boomers in rural Wisconsin tried to look like James Dean and later Boomers aped the Beatles and Stones. I am sure it drove our parents and their friends crazy. But, most of this stuff was cosmetic and today hardly anyone knows what we really looked like and did. Perhaps, best of all, those old police scrapes are not on the internet. Now employers can Google you and read your history of mistakes. They now are available to anyone, forever.

Sexting

I suspect that kids have always been intrigued by the idea of "teasing" each other about sex, but technology has really taken off here. We had Polaroid cameras, but the girls we knew just did not seem interested in giving us nude pictures of them.

When I worked at the US Treasury in the early 1970s, we had a hint of things to come. The International Economics Research Division that I worked for hired some high school interns to work after school and in the summer. Our set of six were all teenage black girls from DC public high schools. They were good kids, and it was a good experience for them (and us). They mostly Xeroxed (yes, Xeroxed—at the time it was the best, no, only technology) and delivered the mail around the building. Even then we didn't trust the government to deliver the government's mail. One day one of our secretaries went to the copy room. We called it going to Florida because the Treasury Building is an old building and, even worse this room did not have much ventilation. It had six powerful and very large Xerox machines churning lots of essential governmental info. Those early Xerox machines generated a lot of heat.

When one of our secretaries opened the door and entered Florida, the interns were Xeroxing their bare butts to give to their boyfriends. As you can imagine, there was a lot of huffing and puffing about what to do about it. No one knew what to do. As a country neighbor we had in Virginia often said, "The wind blew and the shit flew and I couldn't see for an hour or two." Finally, our very smart and sensible boss, The Deputy Assistant Secretary for International Economic Research, "The Deputy Dog," as we called Tom, thought it was harmless and funny and told everyone to forget about it. It stopped there. I am not sure if all the research staff got to see them—okay, of course they did. The important thing is that it stopped with a little embarrassment and a lot of laughing.

Now technology has come a long way, baby. If your kids and grandkids are texting nude pictures of themselves to their girlfriends and boyfriends, they will end up on the internet. Maybe, forever. The same holds for court appearances. Maybe even court appearances because of texting nude photos. In Wyoming County, Pennsylvania, the district attorney is doing just that. He is hauling sexting teens into court. Some of the parents are getting the ACLU to support them against the DA's charges. The parents claim the DA is interfering with their ability to raise their girls "as they see fit." The DA, it is claimed, has violated the girls' freedom of expression. Now that is a good lesson learned. One of the girls whose picture was taken when she was twelve said, "I think the worst punishment is knowing that all you old guys saw me naked. I just think you guys are all just perverts." And even more perverts will have access forever, even perverts in Iran.

What may be even worse is the pseudo intellectual blather they post for the entire world to read. I don't have a face book or whatever. Some of my friends and particularly their kids think this is funny. I have some slightly older friends, one only four years older, who do not do email. I think this is funny, but everything is relative. To email information to them you have to email it to their wives.

I would recommend that you look at what your kids post on the internet. This is NOT like reading their diary. Diary writing is a private endeavor. These innermost thoughts are not intended to be read. If you want to write stupid embarrassing things in a diary when you are young no one else will know how stupid they are. Telling the world things like, "You always have to take in the little things in life" or "Books are good," should probably be kept to yourself. When we were young we probably had some thoughts along these lines, but most of us kept them to ourselves. Maybe we thought someone would punch us in the mouth if we said them. The internet is different; postings are meant to be read.

Take the School Fun Away

Minneapolis schools, and I am sure most others, are banning kids from bringing goodies to school "to spare the feelings of some children whose parents can't afford elaborate treats for the whole class." Let alone protecting the kids with peanut allergies.

Then there is the mother of a second grader who objected that her child was asked to spell "gun" in a school spelling test. I guess she did not want her kid to be able to pass the police school entrance exam. Recently I learned that in the local Minnesota grade school nearby our home the teachers are not allowed to use red pens for fear of offending. Even worse there are no F's. Instead they give the student an NC, which stands for not completed. I guess they will get another crack at completing the material in jail.

Going to College

Soon you will have children and/or grandchildren heading off to college, if they aren't already there. You can help them. Here are few important tips. Test scores and grades matter because they affect where you can get in. One of the reasons that test scores are so important is that high schools are hesitant to give meaningful grades. Look at the numbers. In 1968, 17.6 % of high school students received A's in high school. In 2004, 47.5% of students had an A average. It is likely higher than fifty percent now. That means high school grades are not a very good predictor of potential. So the SAT and ACT allow colleges to better discriminate in admissions. And that is a problem because parents don't like it that their child can't get into any school they want to get into.

Go back to the "my son/daughter is just not a good test taker" argument. I repeat, I call a big BS on that. The problem with that argument is that most kids that give a shit get good grades and do well on tests. Some even get more than one hundred percent on tests. The teachers must not be too good in math if they think there is more than one hundred percent. What this really means is that the teachers are giving high grades to mediocre students and are using extra credit to motivate the brighter students. Whatever! It seems dishonest to me.

These low test scores suggest that students did not learn much. Now that does not mean they can't do well in college, it just means they did not learn shit the last three and one-half years. They could turn it around and learn in college. The SAT and ACT are not aptitude tests. They are for the most part knowledge tests. IQ tests are a better judge of potential. Link a high IQ test score and a low SAT and you have one lazy or uninspired lout. You find this in a lot of boys. If they go to college, and a great teacher turns them on, they can be a true college success.

If kids get a SAT score of above 1500 out of 1600 they can go anywhere and get a lot of scholarships. Tell that to people who tell you SAT scores don't matter. The MD who operated on my cataracts has more than a few kids. We often talk about them and where they are going to college. He told me recently that his experience has taught him that if your kid has at least a 1400 SAT score and you have enough money to be a "full-payer," they can get in anywhere. Full-payer is college admission officer language meaning that you are not looking for student financial aid. Expensive places are perfect discriminators. That means they charge different people different prices to maximize their tuition revenue. They won't admit to it, but they do it. At some prestigious colleges it might even happen that almost everyone but the full payers in the freshman class has paid a different tuition. They do it the same way airlines do it. They separate consumers into different categories. It is even easier for colleges and worse for you, because if you are looking for financial aid you have to fill out their financial forms. This helps them calculate how much they can charge you because they know your income and expenses. The airlines would like the same info if they could figure out how to get it from you. They then could charge you by your ability to pay.

Grades also matter. This is even more the case if the desired college has experience with other kids from the same schools. Most colleges create an index on the high schools they have experience with. No, they will not tell you. It is a secret for good reasons. It may have political, even racial implications. It is a great ranking of both public and private high schools.

This type of data would make an interesting study that would allow school districts to really, I mean really, evaluate a school's value added. You could gather the demographic data on a school district and "predict" the test scores of the students in that district. You could then compare the predicted scores to the actual scores. It may be that some districts have high scores because they have bright kids. Another district with fewer bright or fewer advantaged students may actually be adding more value as measured by test scores. I suggested this to the late Carroll Campbell when he was Governor of South Carolina. He really liked the idea. Even with his help, I was never able to pry the data loose from the South Carolina Department of Education. What do you suppose they were afraid of? Public education is not high on accountability.

It also matters a great deal what you major in. Education students, as a rule, have relatively lower SAT scores and higher grades. Go figure. Also, if you want to teach math, you can't be a math major; you are directed to math courses as in "Math for Teachers." Other students can't take these math for teacher's courses. But math majors, real math majors, who take math courses from math departments will have hell to pay if they want to teach math in grade school or high school. Why? Well, teacher unions have some say in this, as well as colleges of education. Actually, colleges of education are not in the business of teaching new things to students. They are into two things. First, they are certifying new teachers for the union. Secondly, they are training acolytes for changing the world to the global warming, world hunger, world redistribution view of the world. I am not saying this is bad, you decide. I am just telling you this is what is going on.

Engineering majors get jobs. They can do calculus, which means they can figure a lot of things out that others can't, especially education majors. Keep in mind that Isaac Newton invented calculus to solve problems. Every student should learn calculus. In the business school, recruiters will interview Management Science, Accounting, and Finance majors before they will interview Marketing and Management majors. That seems confusing, but it does not need to be. The simple explanation is that the more rigorous, e.g. harder, more quantitative stuff, the better predictor of success it represents. A friend of mine, a former teacher, and a person who read this in an early manuscript, objected to this and argued that social studies and English can be "very hard" for math and engineering majors. But math and engineering students get jobs and English and social studies majors have a much more difficult time finding jobs. Do you need more proof than that? It's what economists call empirical evidence.

How do you feel this kid should be graded?

I have had many friends and relatives tell me that they did not care what their kid majored in, only that they earned a degree. I cringe, but what good would it do for me to tell them they're fools. I already have enough people pissed off at me. I only will repeat this once, if your kid wants to get into a "prestigious" MBA school, they better learn calculus.

I always tell kids that college is fun, but it also an important network for life. All things considered, I would predict that if your son or daughter goes to the best place they can get into, they will do better and have higher quality friends. I joked about stupid commencement speeches when writing about Globaloney, but here is a really insightful one. E. J. Dionne, *Washington Post*, columnist, hit the nail on the head at Wake Forest's 2008 commencement when he said, "To be really affective in life, you really need to know something" (*Chronicle of Higher Education*, July 18, 2008, p. A29).

Pay Scale is a Seattle based company that collects college graduate wage information reported that only 88 US colleges had a return on investment that topped the return on investment of the S&P over the same period. Guess which ones they are: You can come close to guessing them. 1 to 10: MIT, CA. Institute of Technology, Harvard, Harvey Mudd, Dartmouth, Stanford, Princeton, Yale, Notre Dame, and the University of Pennsylvania (*Bloomberg Business Week*, July 4, 2010).

Now don't get depressed. There are ways to overcome bad starts and less opportunity. My favorite economist of all time is the late George Stigler of the University of Chicago. Stigler won the Nobel Prize in Economics in 1982. He was an important player in the Chicago School of Economics. In his autobiography, he stated that the most successful people he had met over the years went to the public university in their state and then to the best graduate school they could get into. So get your kid to go to the University in your state. Not the U sub campus or the U compass campus. By compass I mean Eastern, Western, Southern, or Northern. By sub I mean with a city name that is not the main campus as Madison or Minneapolis. The University of Wisconsin does not refer to itself as the University of Wisconsin, Madison, as does the University of Wisconsin, Stevens Point. Everyone I know who graduated from the University of Wisconsin, Stevens Point, enrolled there after they flunked out of the University of Wisconsin. This does not mean that the U of Xs at wherever of the world are bad places. But buyer beware, they are not THE University. Another very good choice in most states is the Land Grant University. They did not start life as branch campuses. In most states, the land grant engineering program is better than the one at the U, as in Iowa State and Purdue. Sometimes, as in Minnesota and Wisconsin, the U and the Land Grant are the same University. In most other states, the Land Grant is a different university than the U. The Land Grant University is the one with the College of Agriculture and the Agriculture Extension Service, and a great College of Engineering. Clemson, Virginia Tech, and Texas A&M are examples. Sometimes the Land Grant University has state in the title, like Michigan State and Iowa State. After being admitted, get good grades so you can go to any good graduate school you want.

One final point is that if your kid is going to the U, it should be the U in your home state. Out-of-state tuition is pissing money down a U-hole. Unless, of course, you told your kid they could go to school wherever they want if they get good grades. That seems very reasonable to me as long as they get good grades. If kids have good grades and a good SAT, out of state schools will recruit them by offering in-state tuition. That is another reason that test scores are important.

When you drop them off for freshman orientation, they need some advice. Try this on for sage advice. Please feel free to use it.

Go to class. Sit in the first row. Take notes. Spend thirty minutes that day going over your notes after class figuring out what you didn't understand. This should be easy, as you have purchased the textbook. Figure out what confused you. Do this for every class the same day you have that class. You will get A's if you do this. You will be surprised at how little time this takes. Most importantly, you will not have to pull "all-nighters" the night before the exam because you will actually know the material.

You do not need to stop by and "chat-up" your professors. I know your high school teachers have told you that you need to "get to know your teachers." Consider this real life internet student chatting me up in a very recent semester. This is real—I could not make it up. This is the exact email sent in August 2011. "Hello," not hello, Professor or even Mr. or Dr. "My name is: TK I am taking this class so that I can graduate in August 2011. I thought I complete my degree in December 2011 until I just recently was laid off and found out that I needed at least a C in this class to complete my minor. My degree is in: BA CRCJ (that's criminal justice). My hobbies right now since recently been laid off have been just relaxing and reading."

Let me translate this for you. She is a shitty student. Criminal Justice is a weak major. Don't let your kid major in a subject that comes up often when they are introducing the football players on the game of the week. She doesn't think she can get a C in economics and is lobbying for one before the course has even started. The truth is that college faculty hate this bullshit and recognize it is just that.

Let me give you a few more examples from a recent class of mine. I can't pass it up. These are from unedited emails I have recently received from some of my students. I did not make up the spelling and grammar. From JR, a student in my internet eco 1 class. "geeze! im reading the material and it's like chinese to me. im not getting any of it. i took my quiz for chapter 9 and its like i didnt read it. im not getting it. what tips can you offer. seeriously its like a whole other language. crap! i feel im getting behind but i cant grasp it to make a mark on these quizes." So you once thought when you retire you would like to teach college students! My response: "Mr. JR: Please. We have a professional relationship. I am not your buddy. You are a student and I am a Professor. Please refer to yourself as I not i. Is there such a word as geeze? The material is actually written in a different language than your email. It is written in standard English. I would suggest you make use of the tutors in the Economics Department. The last day to drop is July 22. Professor Amacher." I did not hear back from him. Let me translate. This student is really a dumb shit—a rude dumb shit to boot.

Also, don't ask stupid questions. In August this year I got an email from a student, in this case a graduate student, who was enrolling in my five week MBA economics course. It was not scheduled to be taught until November, four months in the future. She asked, "I wanted to inquire about what textbook is required for this course and/or additional materials." Translation, I am brown nosing before the course even starts. I responded, "Do you mean for the course that starts in November?" I didn't hear back. The lesson here is don't draw attention to yourself if you are going to ask stupid questions. Professors know that many students don't read the material when it is assigned and covered. No students read the material ahead of time. Just keep in mind, your professor may seem "strange," many are, but they are not stupid. So even if your high school teacher told you there is no such thing as a stupid question, she was wrong. There are lots of stupid questions. The worst part is they make you look stupid.

Complete your sage advice by telling them to eat healthy, to have dinner. Go out and have a few beers, or whatever mind-expanding substance is in vogue. Meet a lot of new people. Go to a few cultural events to see if you like any of them. It is okay if you don't like them, but this is an inexpensive way to see if you do. They can be very entertaining and fulfilling once you have money of your own. This is an inexpensive way to find out if you like them. If you are taking a theatre class, go work in the theatre. It will help your grade. Meet a lot of new people. If it is your son tell him to try to meet some rich girls, and if it is your daughter tell her to try to meet some rich guys. Join a sorority or a fraternity. This is a good way to meet richer girls and richer guys. Life is easier if your potential spouse comes from a rich family.

Finally, tell them to learn how to concentrate for periods of time. They have been told that a successful skill for their time is multi-tasking. This is

BS. It is rationalization for not being successful. Instead tell them to focus, to concentrate. Do you think Einstein multi-tasked? Sometimes successful people are so focused on something that they seem detached. This is not weird, it is a skill. Finally, don't text while you drive or walk. Recently after class I saw an attractive coed fall down a flight of stairs. She was texting. Yet another example of college as an intelligence test.

Permit me to add a personal pet peeve. Tell them not to ask their professor if there is extra credit available. I know they are used to it in high school. I recently was giving some advice on college majors to one of my wife's cousin's kid, Kirsten, she is a smart, good kid. She proudly told me that she had a 106% average in high school calculus. I told her there is only one hundred percent of anything. I hear these same extra credit questions when I teach economics. It often comes at the end of the semester. My answer is always the same. No. There was plenty of regular credit, just do the assigned work. Extra credit is of interest to two sets of students, those that are brown nosers and those seeking their fifth chance.

Following all this sage advice, hug them; kiss them, on the cheek and say most importantly have a kick-ass time. It is the best time of your life if you follow the simple rules I just gave you. Be safe. And if you get a tattoo, you better major in engineering or find a rich spouse because you are not going to be in our will.

Also tell them to study hard because in four years they are going to be on their own and that includes being on their own health insurance, even if the government has decided you can be on our health insurance until you're 26. Think of the moral hazard associated with this insurance age extension. It puts less pressure on kids to get a job with a company with insurance. This is yet another dimwitted governmental policy that I heard applauded by parents with 25 year old kid/friends who had not yet found a job. It means others will have to pay more. The pool costs will simply go up.

Then get the hell out of there and don't hover. And don't agonize about where all the money is going. You should have thought about that 18 years ago. College is expensive because colleges are very costly to run. There are costly athletic programs to finance. Even athletic programs at colleges that run "minor league" programs are expensive. These lower division programs take in very little income from ticket sales and none from TV revenue. Some programs will tell you that none of the athletic program is funded by tuition. This is mostly BS because as you learned in college, I hope, all budgets are fungible.

Then there are the highly paid administrators. Don't forget the highly paid faculty who get paid get to teach and do research and to do " service." Service is things like serving on committees, and arguing with the administrators about how they are running the college. Faculty at many schools get paid leave. Princeton spends $34K per student on faculty research and takes in about $17K per student in research funding. As they now say, you do the math. Where do you think that money is coming from?

8

Politics and Political Parties

Politics is entertainment for me. It is often outrageously funny. You couldn't make it up. The problem with getting more involved and actually supporting candidates with money or real work is that they almost always disappoint you after they are elected. I once handed out copies of *None Dare Call it Treason* (John Stormer,1964) on a street corner, but that was a long time ago. I also wrote speeches for a Democratic State Senator in South Carolina, and that was fun. He always read these speeches when he gave them, most of them for the first time. He was chair of the South Carolina Senate Finance Committee. That made it great fun. Hey, he trusted me. More importantly, he was a sensible South Carolina Democrat. Hopefully, he was more sensible because he trusted me.

In the spirit of truth in writing about politics, I should start by being forthright with my biases. This is in stark contrast with most writers, particularly members of the press. The worst of them claim that they are independent, but they mostly spew support for liberal causes. Very few, and those are mostly on Fox, are right of center, even fewer are libertarian. They are also on Fox. My friends referred to CNN as the Clinton News Network during his eight years in office. Even the great Walter Cronkite provided cover for Bill Clinton during MonicaGate. The picture of Walter sailing with his wife, Hillary, Chelsea, and Bill was again prominent in NBC's coverage of Cronkite's recent death. This action depreciated the value of his memory for me.

I started reading politics in *The Milwaukee Journal* as a kid. *The Milwaukee Journal* had a four page insert called "The Green Sheet." It was printed on light green paper and it was four pages of comics. Now that was a great marketing technique. I suspect the "Green Sheet" had a lot to do with getting kids to read the paper. I am afraid that many newspapers will soon disappear. There are some good, mostly economic reasons for their demise, but more on why later. Back to full political disclosure.

My personal belief is that there are really only two Presidents in my lifetime that were worth a shit. I have to exclude Ike because I was a bit too young to make an informed judgment. I don't think he did "too much" so that would put him high on my list. I also am careful with JFK, because his "best and brightest" rewrote so much of his history to protect his legacy, and theirs. *The Best and Brightest* (Ballentine 1969) is the term that David Halberstam coined in his book with the same title for all the pointy-headed Harvard intellectuals Kennedy brought to Washington with him. Robert McNamara is notable in this group. He spent the rest of his life trying to defend a good place in history for himself.

In my earlier Boomer years, I was drawn to both JFK and RFK. I was beginning to understand some economics and what they said struck me as mostly sensible. JFK's rise is an interesting story. Their father, Joseph P. Kennedy, was a successful businessman, starting in the saloon business and moving on to import Scotch before prohibition ended. He ended up as the US Ambassador to Britain. His term came to a quick end when he published some controversial remarks that democracy was finished in England and this could happen in the US. That argument strikes me as pretty insightful. Without Margaret Thatcher, he would have been right and you can't blame him for not anticipating the rise of that great lady. Papa Kennedy saw the trends early and read them correctly.

Later, some of these same best and brightest pointy heads made Ted Kennedy the torch bearer for JFK and RFK, and portrayed him as a great leader. He mostly didn't make sense to me and he certainly made very bad, risky, some might even say immoral decisions under pressure. If JFK had not been shot, my guess is Ted would never have been elected to the US Senate. Both President Kennedy and even more, Senator Robert Kennedy, made sense to me in what they said about economic issues and even some political issues. They were much more centrist than national Democrats are today. Robert seemed to have had a better understanding of economics than most politicians. Even more, Robert was more on the free market side of issues than most Democrat candidates. The week after Teddy's funeral, I was amused to read that at least one other Minnesota reader of *The Star Tribune* newspaper understood the differences between Ted and his older brothers. "I can't help but think that when Ted, RFK, and JFK are united in heaven, eventually the conversation will get around to Jack asking his brother, 'Dude, what did you do with my party?'" (Alex Adams-Leytes, September 29, 2009.)

I was amused because this made it into the "Red Star" and it was written by a man with a hyphenated last name. It is the most insightful thing I have ever read by a hyphenated last name male in this liberal rag. Maybe I will renew my subscription.

Reading recently about the fact that he was doing Jackie has not changed my feelings about RFK. This behavior must have been part of the Kennedy family DNA. There was a report in the summer that the widow of the man buried in a crypt in California was removing his body and auctioning off the crypt on e-Bay. He was buried in the place just above Marilyn Monroe, facing downward. You couldn't make it up. On the same level and next to Monroe is Hugh Hefner's spot for eternity. The bidding was reported to be above $3 million. If the Kennedys weren't such important markers to us Boomers, I might be tempted to suggest the feds use some stimulus money to buy the crypt and move the Kennedy brothers to be "with" Marilyn. That would really be a shovel ready project. They both were certainly attracted to her in life, as she was to them.

I was surprised, but I found myself emotionally moved, during the news coverage surrounding the death of Ted Kennedy. I was surprised by this because I did not like his politics very much at all. My emotion must have been because of the Boomer marker from 1963 still tugging on me. It was repeated over and over by the members of the Senate club that talked about him, that he was a congenial opponent. Senator Ted Kennedy must have been a good guy in the locker room, as even his senate opponents certainly seemed to like him. I would bet he could tell a great sex joke. But I don't think the great Vince Lombardi would buy into such a definition of competition. I came away thinking that it was maybe a good thing that John McCain lost. He might have supported Senator Kennedy's health care bill just because they were friends. The recent arguments that they all need to work together and be civil is a bit disturbing to me.

My problem with McCain when he was the Republican presidential candidate was that I could never determine a consistent philosophy in his positions. As a Senator, he often wanted to look into issues that were not the business of government. One example was drug use in sports. If this is an important issue, sports leaders should look into it. The federal government would, I hope, have more serious issues to look into. Maybe I have this wrong; maybe we would be better off if they looked into things that don't matter, like sports, and left the important things, like health care, alone.

While I listened to the moving family tributes it struck me how different the rich are and how differently the rich and privileged grow up. The rich learn sailing to teach discipline and competitiveness. When I was a kid, I watered mink on Jack Bauer's mink ranch. Watering mink is an important mink farm task as mink are water animals and they need a lot of water to drink and splash around in. Mink, at least in captivity, smell awful and their odor permeates your clothes as they piss on you and your clothes. It is an all around shit job but it taught me some discipline as I knew I needed to get the hell out of there. Very similar concept, different income levels.

The young Kennedys practiced tacking long into the night with Uncle Ted so they could win the scheduled Regatta at their, I am sure, fancy sailing club. Until recently, I didn't know anyone who grew up sailing at a sailing club. All the kids I knew grew up learning their discipline and honed their competitiveness in summer and after school jobs. Also, of course, on the playground. Maybe we could have a big impact on the poor if we had governmentally provided sailing schools. Maybe the poor could be sent to summer camp on Martha's Vineyard to learn how to compete more effectively. And it could be part of a future stimulus package. I am sure it is shovel ready, but I am not sure if the sailing clubs or for that matter the rich liberal folks in Martha's Vineyard want poor kids hanging around. Rich folks are firmly in the NIMBY crowd when it comes to the poor.

I digress. Let me get back to politics. I think the two greatest presidents of our Boomer years have been Ronald Reagan and Bill Clinton. I will try to explain this seemingly conflicting statement.

Many if not most of my political soul mates are what I would call conservative/libertarians. By that I mean they really think people should be left alone by government and meddlesome politicians. They are pro choice; they don't care about who or what you want to marry; think drugs should be legalized; think taxes should be lower; understand evil in the world and the necessity of a strong defense; think stem cell research is a good idea if it is not carried out by the government; think unions have excessive influence because of their coziness with some state and local governments and the Democrat party. Mostly we think that government is not good at doing much. The net result of these beliefs is that most of us think that less government is better than more government. We think the US Post Office is an old concept. We have learned the important lesson that private for profit firms do a very good job of delivering stuff to our houses. FEMA demonstrates, once again, that government is not very good at doing things. It was the Post Office delivering disaster assistance. We worry about health care in the future when it may be delivered by doctors and nurses in blue uniforms with a patch on the sleeve. Maybe we will even call them Medmen. The head of the hospital then would be the Medmaster. Then maybe Fed Ex and UPS would go into the health care business and put the whole health care debate to rest. It was recently reported that the Feds lost many of the bodies of dead soldiers in Arlington National Cemetery. Do you think they could keep track of patients who can move about? Back to Bill.

I like Bill Clinton because of his commitment to freer world trade. This is a difficult position for a Democrat. The farmer and union constituencies of traditional Democrats do not like freer trade. Clinton seemed to instinctively understand that the free trade agreements were not "great sucking sounds," sorry Ross Perot. Maybe Clinton "knew" great sucking sounds. He understood that freer trade caused more growth for folks in all countries. Maybe he took economics in college and learned something. Maybe he just listened to his economists. He had some good ones and this is a point that almost all economists agree on. The few economists that don't agree with this truism work for labor unions or the auto industry. While free trade is sometimes not good for certain segments of the economy, overall it was good because it causes per capita GDP to rise in both exporting and importing countries. GDP is gross domestic product, which is all the goods and services added up in a single number. If it goes up in both exporting and importing countries that is a good thing. It means people in both countries have more goods and services to consume. Economists call this a positive sum gain. The simple fact is that if both parties in a market transaction are not made better off, the trade would not take place.

Clinton finessed the unions on this issue. He would campaign in Detroit telling the union workers that he would help them. He did this by coyly implying that he would not support NAFTA extensions. But he supported agreements that made world trade grow. The press called it his ability to "triangleize." I understood this to mean promising to do one thing and doing something else. As in political lying or what some of my friends call normal campaign trail "speech a-fyin.'" The Congressman from South Carolina was shouting the truth when he called President Obama a liar during the State of the Union Speech. He was correct and at the same time disrespectfully impolite. When I lived in

South Carolina it seemed that to me South Carolinians were first and foremost polite. I choose to think it was political frustration because I wager he is polite.

Susan practicing a modern version of duck and cover.

The Republican Party presents a difficult case for coalition building. You have what I call the Country Club Republicans. They aren't much different than Democrats. Many of them want things from government. Others don't like free trade. They think they are different from Democrats. Mostly they think they could do a better job of running government than traditional Democrats because they are businessmen. They are not opposed to big government. They just think they can manage it better. Nelson Rockefeller was the poster boy of this wing of Republicanism. I think I would also put Jerry Ford is this group. They think people matter more than policies about less government. Some of them are smart and successful, but they don't have an understanding of the impotence of government. Mitt Romney probably fits here. He thinks he can run government because he managed the Olympics. Puke. The Olympics mostly get an unlimited subsidy from NBC. Maybe Mitt could get NBC to sponsor the federal government. That is as silly as alleging that the Olympic experience is relevant for the Presidency.

These folks say nonsensical things like, "Government needs to work more like business." Government can't work like business because it is government. We all know it can't because there are different incentives in government than in business. Have you ever heard of a business mandating earmarks?

Next you have the Libertarians who understand that it is the government that is the problem. They want government to be smaller and really would not care who runs it, if it is small enough. The Religious Right, the ministerial wing of the party, has nothing in common with Libertarians. This makes it seem to me next to impossible to put a meaningful coalition together. The Religious Right is almost anti-libertarian. They want to tell you how to live your life. If you need both groups to get along to win an election, it seems to me to be next to impossible. Many of them would rather lose than form a winning coalition. "We will just stay home on election day," is their battle cry.

Both Reagan and Clinton were masterful coalition builders. Then after they won, they concentrated attention on successful economic policies. The interesting part of their coalition building is that the coalitions were not natural. And importantly, they both did it twice. Reagan included the Religious Right, but ignored their agenda. Bill Clinton put together a coalition that included labor unions, blue collar workers, the minority community, academics, Hollywood, and the liberal establishment, and talked their agenda day and night. Clinton then expanded trade so aggressively that many of the other costs of government were overwhelmed by the economic power of freer trade. The real threat of Democrat presidents is the trade issue and the growth of government issue. And one more time, Bill Clinton was a genius at finessing this issue. My wife thinks that Dick Cheney is the third best President in our Boomer set of Presidents. He made her feel safe. She may be right on the President point.

Political Parties

It seems to me that we need some new parties, like the "Freedom Lovers and Economic Growth Facilitators." That would be the smaller government folks and include the Libertarians. It most likely would have room for Boomer Catholics as they have been ignoring papal statements they don't like since they were kids. It would also include those voters who think the world is full of bad people who make it a dangerous place for freedom loving people. Maybe Newt Gingrich could be the Chair of this new Party. He has a lot of good ideas and would likely take the job. He must understand that he is not electable in a national election. He has a disagreeable voice and the Religious Right, except for maybe Governor Sanford of South Carolina, doesn't approve of his past life style issues. If Newt isn't interested, maybe Dick Cheney's daughter could take it on as she really makes sense on important issues and as the daughter of a former President, she has status. We could call this party the "Libercans." They might use a mammoth as a symbol.

The other party would be the European style socialism lovers. These are the folks that really think European democracies work better than the US works. These politicians are trying to be more like Sweden and Norway at the same time that some sensible politicians in Sweden and Norway are trying to be less like Sweden and Norway. They would be known as the "Controlacrats" and use Mr. Ed as their symbol. Colin Powell could be their founding Chair. One term President Barach Obama could be their spokesperson.

The only group that would be left out of these two new parties is the Religious Right. Reverend Huckabee could be their candidate. He makes a lot of sense on some important issues, but the Religious Right is the anti-Libertarian party. They are anti-Libertarian because they do not want to allow you to make your own decisions on many important matters that are none of their god damn business. If I could only see Reverend Huckabee crossing his fingers behind his back one time, I might change my feeling about his electability and be able to support him. To his credit, I really think he believes what he says and that means I could never vote for him. I cannot vote for a candidate of the Religious Right that really believes the agenda. This is because I believe God to be a libertarian. It's that Grace thing I brought up before. It is, in fact, my working definition of Grace. To me it is an attitude stated simply as if you don't like abortion or drug use, or guns, or whatever your single issue, you forgive them for not knowing what they do and get on with your own life.

I would suggest Colin Powell as chair of the Controlocrats, in large part, because his inconsistency confuses me. He has always claimed to be a Republican, but then he bolted and supported Obama. I think he used the Republican Party for affirmative action. He is a poster person for successful affirmative action in America. He was an Army officer. The US Military is the best early example of affirmative action that worked. He was then plucked out of the military by Republicans and moved through increasingly important positions until he became Secretary of State. He then bolted to support President Obama. He forgot those who helped him most. This is reprehensible to me.

When we lived in Crested Butte, Colorado, we knew many couples who had spent a lot of time in Europe. A good number of the men were married to European women they had met when they worked for corporate America in Europe. Many nights over dinner and drinks, and drinks and sometimes more drinks, we discussed politics. Very often they were critical of Reagan and Bush, the elder. They all thought that the only person that was capable in these Republican administrations was Colin Powell. Who turns out to have been a make believe Republican. Needless to say we had some fun evenings. Actually, Colin Powell fits into the Country Club Republican cubby hole. Like Nelson Rockefeller, he thinks government would work just fine if he were running it. That makes sense, as he is a product of the US Army. The late Warren Nutter, an expert on the Soviet Union and a teacher of mine in graduate school, always said, "If you want to understand the problems of central planning you can study the Department of Defense." At the time it was the second largest planned economy in the world and had all the problems of Soviet style economic planning. Colin Powell would, for that matter, see himself as Commander General of the US.

Dopey Politicians

Most Boomers who are truthful will admit to having smoked dope, or weed, or doobies, or whatever it was called at the time. This became a problem when these same Boomers entered politics. I remember way back when Bruce Babbitt of Arizona, who was born in 1938, making him six years too old to be a Boomer, first committed the dope "mistake" while campaigning in the early Iowa presidential caucuses. He was asked if he had ever smoked dope in college. He admitted that he had. The press had a field day. President Clinton, acute observer of history that he is, answered the same question by saying that he had, but that "he didn't inhale." George W. Bush danced around the question, and got a lot of press that no one seemed to pay much attention to. It finally just went away. However history ultimately treats President Obama, he should at least get credit for putting an end to this stupid question. He was asked a la Bill

Clinton if he had ever inhaled. His response was something like "that was the purpose wasn't it?" That simple response ended this question forever, we can hope. Candidate Obama has driven a stake in the heart of that issue. I always thought it was a voter intelligence test, rather than a candidate intelligence test. Who would vote for a candidate, or most importantly, a Boomer candidate that had not even tried it?

Stimulate Us

The politics of recessions are curious. President Obama won in a landside in large part because voters blamed Bush II for the economic crisis. The new administration quickly set out to stimulate the economy out of this "deep" recession. It was arguably the worst recession since the Great Depression. It was however different than the Great Depression. The stock market did not plunge nearly as far and unemployment didn't rise nearly as high. In fact, unemployment did not rise as high as it did in the Jimmy Carter recession. And Carter's recession was never compared to the Great Depression. The Carter recession was scary enough for us Boomers because none of us personally remembered the Great Depression. After all we were born after WWII. What we remember is the endless and utter meaningless references to it from our parents. Often this was said to us in such useless terms as, "eat your beets, we would have been happy to have beets in the depression." It was a real marker on their generation, so much so that they never seemed to let go of it.

WWII was the primary reason we got out of the Great Depression. I am not suggesting we go to war, although I must admit to being amused by Senator McCain's take on the Beach Boy's version of "Barbara Ann." What I am suggesting is that the huge spending policy of FDR did not get us out of the Great Depression. War got us out because the factories were busy building tanks and airplanes and the unemployed men went into the military. At the start of the war the unemployment rate was high. Yet the general public takes it for granted that the Keynesian based fiscal policy of FDR ended the Great Depression.

My wife's cousin, Randi, has a daughter, Erica, who was in junior high school in Arizona last year. On a visit to Minnesota she and her mother stopped at our house to chat. This junior high school student was telling us what a great year she had in school with a great social studies teacher that taught them that

FDR ended the Great Depression. She went on to say that President Obama would do the same because he was doing the same things President Roosevelt did. Child abuse I say. Maybe child abuse is too strong a word. It is more like re-education, a la Mao. The last thing some know-nothing public school teacher should be doing is teaching economics. I bet she learned that in a college course on how to teach social studies by a college of education professor. I guarantee you she did not learn it from an economics professor.

Even President Obama played this game. Shortly after he became president, he announced his stimulus plan and said he had not met an economist that did not agree with it. Two days later, the Cato Institute published a statement signed by many economists, including three Nobel Prize winners that started with the words, "With All Due Respect Mr. President, We Disagree." I'm number two on the list and proud to be listed with such distinguished economists. This was the first time I liked it that my name began with an A. I did not like it when I was a kid or when I was in the Army. When I was in parochial grade school I hated it that my name started with an A. It meant I had to sit within a ruler's distance of Miss (not Ms.) Opitz. At least I thought that was the reason. Miss Opitz was the Lutheran equivalent of a nun teaching in the Lutheran day school. She was my third and fourth grade teacher. She also had been my mother's third and fourth grade teacher. German Lutheran teachers were slow to change and didn't retire.

The public demanded action on the economy and we got it. Oh did we get it. The liberal wing of the Democrat party wanted to do programs and the need for a stimulus package is a good way to expand government programs. But keep in mind that it is not the only way to stimulate the economy. We could cut taxes. The Air Force could fly around the country and drop money out of planes. People fortunate enough to be under those planes could scoop up the money and spend it. They could pay off their mortgages, buy a new car, or pay their college tuition. You get the idea. The thing to look at closely is who is doing the spending and what it is being spent on. Politicians would not like the idea of a money air drop. Politicians like programs so they get credit with certain constituencies for helping them. Besides, politicians think people would spend the money on the "wrong things," like boats, tuition for their kids, or even good gin. So we got a program focused on clunkers. This appealed to liberal types because it is argued it was good for the environment.

Cash for Clunkers

The Cash for Clunkers program, a part of Obama's stimulus plan, received high praise from many folks. The press, for the most part labeled it a win—win program. You need to be careful when you see something praised as win—win. Win—win things have already been done. In situations where every participant wins, private exchange takes place. That is the essence of free exchange. Both sides get something they want. Remember opportunity cost. Somebody has to be paying for this program. When politicians say win—win what they really are saying is that they know what is best and that stupid folks can't figure these things out, even those who lose.

Cash for Clunkers offered people up to $4,500 off the price of a more fuel efficient car. The money would be rebated by the Feds to the car dealers. The car dealers had to fill out a lot of paperwork and wait a long time to get money the Feds promised. It is estimated that about 625,000 cars were sold under this program and the dealers got about $3,000,000,000 in federal stimulus money. Who are the winners? Well, clearly the folks who got a car for $4,500 less than they would have are winners. What about the auto dealers? If people purchased cars that they would not have without the Cash for Clunkers program, the auto dealers won. How many sales are these? This is really hard to determine. How many of these purchasers would have purchased a car in 2010 or 2011, but speeded that purchase up. Greenies thought they gained because Clunkers were pollution machines that used a lot of gas. I was surprised when I learned that the answer here is "not so much." The program was over-hyped. *Business Week* calculated that the gas savings of the Clunkers program was about fifty six million gallons or .04% of US consumption. That is .04% not 4% or even .4%. The reduction in CO_2 emissions was also calculated to be .04%.—I repeat .04%. This is pretty expensive fuel efficiency and CO_2 reduction, but then the people who were buying these cars did not pay for that. Who did? You're right you smart SOB, you did. In other words, it may have been a win-win for some folks but it was a big lose-lose for you. It was also a big loss for the charity programs that rely on gifts of cars. "Cars for Kids" is a program that accepts cars, fixes them up, and auctions them off. The proceeds are used to teach the kids how to repair cars and learn a marketable skill. I gave them a Clunker two years ago and was impressed with their program. Their charity is sucking hind tit now.

It was also a loss for the mechanics that could have been hired to keep the older cars in running shape. Now the dealers are worried that another slump is on the way because the Clunkers program mostly shifted future demand into the rebate period producing very poor current sales present.

I talked to a car dealer friend weeks after the program ended. He said his dealerships were financially hanging out, because of the long delay in getting the Clunker checks from the government. The money finally came about two months after the program ended. Government can't even figure out how to get the promised money to the dealers. Maybe dropping money out of airplanes is an attractive, less discriminatory alternative. Less discriminatory in the sense that the government would not be choosing the winners.

More help quickly followed. A new program labeled in *The Wall Street Journal* as "Cash for Dishwashers," came to appliance stores in your state. This program, funded with "only"$300 million, was different, because each state could determine the amount of cash for the machines. Not only can each state determine the amount of the rebate, it can also pick the models that qualify. What could be next?

Cash for Lunkers

Folks in Minnesota were big losers. They need a better targeted program. If only Al Franken would have been seated earlier we might have had a "Cash for Walleyes" program. Walleyes over 17.5 inches would earn a $4,500 rebate check from the Feds. No, let's make this a more general stimulus package. The more general the program the fairer it would be. Why should we discriminate in favor of walleye fishermen and against catfish fishermen? God, there may even be some racial aspects to this. Most Walleye fisherman have blue eyes. If there were "fishing organizers" they would be flying in to protest. You can see how difficult policy making is. It should be, no, it must be a general program. Any fish over 17.5 inches would qualify as a lunker and we would call it the "The Cash for Lunkers" federal stimulus program. Fisherman would of course gain because they would receive the checks. Boat makers would gain because interest in fishing would increase. Boat dealers would gain for the same reason. Likewise for fishing pole and bait makers. Fishing guides would see increased demand for their services. Kids could dig up worms and make money for back to school stuff. Restaurant and bar owners in the fishing areas would gain. This is really a bar friendly program as we all know about fishing and drinking. State tax revenue from fishing license fees and drunk driving fines would go up. I better stop there, but I think I have just hit the tip of this economic growth machine. The ripple effects with this program, maybe we should use the term wake effects, could go on forever. The politicians would call this a win-win. Sorry, again taxpayers would be losers. Those car dealers would lose because this program blesses a different group of consumers. They would not have a program that "blessed" them, unless, of course, the dealers were also fishermen, or boat dealers. This is getting complicated. Oh shit, we have just seen that the losers in the Cash for Clunkers program are almost all of us. How depressing. No wonder the Tea Party folks are finding traction.

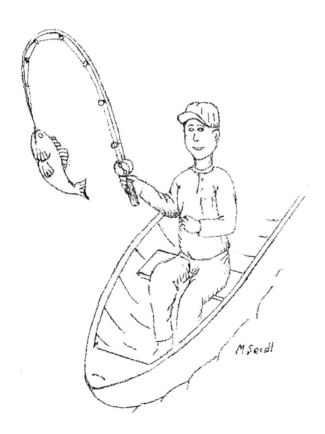

A Rod and Reel Ready Program.

Now you may think that a program like Cash for Lunkers is crazy, maybe even funny. Consider some Minnesota alternatives. The Minnesota State Arts Board is considering how to spend the $316,200 federal stimulus money "earmarked for the arts." The competing proposals include $25K for the Flying Foot Forum, a Minneapolis dance group, a non-specified amount for the TVbyGirls, no purpose specified either, and $15K for the Twin Cities Gospel Choir; so much for the separation of church and state. These programs make Cash for Lunkers seem reasonable.

How did we end up with all this mumbo jumbo? Well, it was clear that whoever was elected President we were going to get a big stimulus. There not a dime's worth of difference between the candidates on stimulus issues, except, of course, on which interest groups benefited most. It mostly just had to be bigger than what Bush II was pursuing. Remember McCain was a candidate who thought government can solve a lot of problems. He liked to poke his nose in a lot of stuff as a senator. He is most likely one of the Country Club Republicans, by that I mean rich white folks. His big bucks came to him via marriage, but Country Club Republicans don't care where ones' wealth comes from, except in private.

But consider some simple alternatives. On one end of the spectrum, if you were elected President you could ask your economists to give you a number about the size of a stimulus they thought was needed. You could then send checks to people or do a cash flyover. At one extreme, you could ask the IRS to give you the names of everyone who filed a tax form last year. You could use that number as the denominator and the number your economists gave you as the numerator. You could then cut checks to every taxpayer. Or you could cut tax rates. Na, that's too simple and on top of that, no politicians could take credit for creating shovel ready projects. They would all want to spend it on projects to stimulate the economy. Or, you could appoint a stimulus chief, maybe even give the job to the Secretary of the Treasury, and let him spend the money. You could pay off some of the people that elected you. You could pay off ACORN. You could pay off whomever you wanted to win over. You could build a bridge to nowhere in every state. Or maybe just in the states where you won the electoral votes. Is this fun or what? Being President is a lot like being Santa Claus and you don't have to live at the North Pole with height challenged assistants.

All this governmental activity costs a great deal of money. No, a very great deal of money. It appears that the stimulus package is going to add about $9 trillion to the deficit. That $9,000,000,000,000 figure came from Obama Administration Officials in September, 2009. I hate it when just an official is being quoted. No official wants their name associated with that high a figure. And it will go higher. Bet on that. It was pointed out the previous estimate of $7,100,000,000,000 was an underestimate because of the sluggish recovery. The $7,100,000,000,000 would have been the largest deficit in history and the largest as a percent of GDP since the end of WWII. The money was intended to solve the problem of the sluggish economy. I guess the unnamed official was admitting failure. That is another good reason to be unnamed. And I remember President Obama saying, even recently, that he was going to cut the deficit by the end of his first term. Instead, it has grown by $2,000,000,000,000. That is almost 30% higher than the President's economists predicted. If you want to wager it will not go even higher, please call me.

How do you know when any US President is lying? The answer is: when he is promising to reduce the size of the budget deficit. I keep thinking back to what I heard economist Art Laffer, of the Laffer curve fame, say on Fox. The "Laffer Curve" was an easy way to understand description of supply side economics. It was a graph that showed you could decrease tax rates and tax revenue could increase.

Laffer reported that he once told President Reagan that the person most responsible for Reagan winning the presidency was Jimmy Carter. He also said that Reagan was amused. This history shows that President Obama does not have much time to end the recession if he wants to keep from becoming a one-term president.

Health Care

Health care in the US is the best in the world. It is hard to believe this truth if you listen to the political rhetoric coming out of Washington. President Obama recently called for a "truthful" debate on health care. He insisted that he is truthful and the opposition is lying. Let's use the old turnstile theory of government. Imagine that every person in the world can go to any country for medical services. We would judge the best medical services to be the ones that informed sick people want to patronize. It is just like good restaurants or high quality car production. Medical care is, if anything, more sensitive to this movement because people with serious medical issues are better informed about where there is high quality care. They have every incentive to become informed because the cost of a wrong decision could be very high. It could be a life or death decision. Where do people from all over the world with money go when they are really sick? They go where they can buy the Rolls Royce of medical care. They come to the US. Now why would we want to destroy this system of health care?

Middle class (not rich—middle class) Canadians, who often brag about the Canadian version of socialized health care, plan their visits to the medical service industry when they are at their Florida "winter home." My wife's cousin, Kari, who lived in Norway as she was married to a Norwegian, always planned her "medical services" to coincide with her visits back to Minnesota.

Ignorance of the way markets work and the role they play is, of course, one of the reasons that public health care is considered a basic right. But let's be careful here. There are a lot of well-meaning people that think we should have socialized medicine. I don't have any friends that feel that way, or if they do they keep it to themselves because they know how I would react. I do have acquaintances and relatives that think we need public medicine. We actually do have "socialized" parts of US medicine. Military hospitals and veterans hospitals are an example of post office medicine. Remember the scandals two years ago about how bad some of these military hospitals were and the calls to fix them fast. Then remember we learned the feds can't keep track of the dead bodies in Arlington Cemetery. How can we expect them to keep track of soldiers who are moving about, however imperfectly?

Hospitals on Indian reservations in the US are another good example of Government Health Care. The Indian Health Service provides US Public health care to American Indians and Alaska natives. Terry Anderson, in *The Wall Street Journal*, August 29, 2009, found that life expectancy on a South Dakota Indian Reservation was 58 years. The average for all Americans is 77. So much for the quality of the governmental health care programs. Apologists will argue that Native Americans have a high incidence of smoking and alcoholism. Some even say that Native American genes are predisposed to addiction. Maybe they get drunk because they have such piss poor governmental health care. And the same is true for poor fat Americans of all races and colors. That makes public health care more unworkable. Healthiness requires a great deal of personal discipline and wise choice making. Government is not good at fostering either personal or wise choice making.

The United Kingdom has had universal health care for more than 60 years, the longest period of socialized medicine in the free world. Not coincidentally, the UK is by far the most unpleasant place to be ill in the Western World. "Even Greeks living in Britain return home for medical treatment, if they are physically able to do so," Theodore Dalrymple, *The Wall Street Journal*, July 29, 2009, A13. Check mate.

Who makes these pro public health care arguments? Some are made by people who are concerned about the poor not getting their fair share or even adequate health care because many of the poor are not insured. At the most basic level, this is not an argument about health care. It is an argument about wealth redistribution. It is an argument for the redistribution of income. The poor don't have most things as good as the rich. That would include cars, homes, wine. Almost everything the poor have is inadequate when compared to what the rich have. That is what it means to be poor. If we carried this to an extreme, everyone would have to have the same goods and services and the same quality of goods and services. Sounds kind of like Marx, and we all (should) know that did not work very well.

Fundamentally, at the most basic level, Barack Obama's health care plan is about rationing scarce medical service. President Obama said when his health bill passed Congress in early 2010 that it was essentially identical to the health care legislation Mitt Romney signed in Massachusetts four years earlier. Most Republicans disagreed with the President's plan and opposed it. The Massachusetts Plan is starting to show results. There have been price controls placed on insurance rate increases. There has been runaway spending and limits placed on health care. Proponents of the Obama plan deny this and say that there will be no limits on care for any individual. No one is going to decide when Grandma is going to die. But the Econ 1 of it is that if you are going to supply service through the government at below market prices, someone is going to decide who gets them. Kari, the same cousin from Norway, told me about a friend of hers in Lillehammer who had three children and was still young. She went to make an appointment to have her "tubes tied." The queue was 4 years long. She flew to the US to have the surgery. And if grandpa gets prostate cancer at age 75, it makes no economic sense to give him expensive treatment. Send him to the end of the queue and he will be dead before he gets to the front.

Here is where the Kevorkian question rears its head again. I saw Kevorkian on the Neil Cavuto show on Fox shortly before his death and he seemed like a person who had given a great deal of thought to the assisted death concept. He made it clear that he never got involved with anyone who did not express a coherent desire to die. These were very sick, suffering people, many with Lew Gehrig's disease, a very "difficult" way to die.

Old people are going to die. One more time, this time with sympathy and understanding—as death gets nearer problems develop that are sometimes not related to the disease, but are at the core of the reason death is nearing. For many, if not most folks, this means breathing becomes more difficult. They are intubated. If they have difficulty eating, a feeding tube is implanted, even if they can't swallow or are not interested in food. If their heart stops, they are resuscitated. In fact, statistics show that if treatment is stopped in a terminally ill patient they die on average only 29 days earlier than those kept in a critical care unit. These are very expensive days and they have a high opportunity cost. Perhaps, most importantly the quality of life is very, very low. These resources cannot be used to keep someone alive who might recover. Simple economics— the opportunity cost of choices, hard choices.

Earlier, I talked about getting to know the wishes of your parents and how important it is to enforce their choices if they do not wish to be kept alive. A hospice can be important here, but, you have to be strong to support these wishes. Think how wonderful it would be if you could make these decisions for yourself.

When we are talking about public options, we are really talking about the redistribution of income, Robin Hood type taking and giving. This is a difficult topic that has important impacts on incentives. Let me try a simple example. The first question is do we want ex post or ex ante equity. This is Latin for equity before the fact or equity after the fact. This is not a difficult concept. Think of it as the hundred meter dash in the Olympics. Do we want the race to be fair by forcing all runners to start at the time the gun goes off, and if someone jumps the gun, to bring all the runners back to restart? Or do we want all the runners to cross the finish race at the same time? If we forced all runners to finish the race at the same time, how much do you think runners would train? Is that a fair question? Of course it is. Lou Holtz recently tested the wind for a try at an open Congressional race. In one interview, he was talking about the lack of competitiveness among young folks. He argued that one reason for this lack of competitiveness is that every kid gets a trophy for participating. This seems so fundamental, but it is an issue that many people don't understand. Perhaps they don't want to understand.

Watching the funeral of Ted Kennedy, I was struck by the fundamental difference between equality of opportunity and equality of outcome. A clip showing Senator Kennedy giving a speech shortly after first being elected to the Senate was repeated often. In the speech, he said and I am paraphrasing, "When I came to this August Body, I came with the idea that the rich and privileged need to make the playing ground even for the poor." I can't say I have ever met anyone who would disagree with that concept. Does this mean bringing those who jump the gun back and starting the race over or does it mean making sure everyone finishes the race at the same time. The difficulty with big government is that those running government end up promoting the latter because they can't figure out what do with those who don't take advantage of an equal start. Or perhaps even more basic, they don't like the outcomes when they work to ensure equal opportunity, because not everyone trains as hard as they need to. What do you do with those who don't train? These are very difficult conversations because those who disagree are often charged with being racists. Bill Cosby has been out front in some of these discussions and even he has taken heat for doing so. If a white man said what Bill Cosby says, Attorney General Holder would call him a racist.

Incentives are what markets are all about. These market incentives are powerful and if you alter incentives, behavior changes. Even in the socialist democracies, i.e., the Commie countries, everyone did not get the same things. The party members had far better cars and clothes. They lived in nicer houses and even shopped for food in different stores. Often their housing and shopping areas were hidden from view so that workers did not know.

Almost everyone wants to help the poor, the sick, the old, and the handicapped get some redistribution, some help. The real question is about how much and for how long? That determines how much we slow the fastest runners down. These are thorny questions. The closer we get to everyone finishing the race at the same time, the more likely no one will want to train to race. Consider some options. We could decide a certain "basic needs" budget for medical care and we could transfer income to those below that need. We could do it through a negative income tax. A negative income tax simply transfers income to the poor and allows them to make their own economic decisions.

This would require individuals to make the right decisions themselves. Many big government liberals will object to this on the grounds that the poor will make bad decisions. This is arrogant bull shit and shows what low regard these liberals have for those they want to help.

Some hard decisions will have to be addressed. Let me suggest a few of them. Should obese sick people get health care transfers? Many poor people and children in America are obese. "Obesity cost US businesses $45 billion per year in business expense and lost productivity" (*Business Week*, February 23, 2009, p.7). It is reported that twenty six percent of Americans are obese. The biggest problems are in the South. Colorado has the lowest rates when ranked by state. Twenty percent of 4 year olds are obese. The numbers by nationality are Asians 13%, Whites 16%, Blacks 21% Hispanics 22%, and American Indians 31%. Should we say, if you are obese and/or smoke, you are not qualified for assistance, unless the disease is producing the obesity rather than the obesity causing or contributing to the disease?

Hardly anyone gives a damn about smokers, so I guess we could just let them die in the street, which is where they have to go to smoke anyway. You can see how difficult this becomes. In England, if you have a heart issue and you smoke you go to the end of the health care service line—sorry, queue. If we have government financed transplants, should obese people go to the end of the line? Fear not, if you are fat. The Surgeon General is enough overweight to be classified as obese and she will be making the rules. I don't know if she smokes. Maybe she has an occasional "heater" with the President.

This poor and fat issue is uniquely found in the modern developed countries. Almost everywhere else in the world, poor people are skinny, often malnourished. The well-fed look is for the rich. Historically, in the US, the wealthier were fatter than poorer, working people. Newspaper cartoons in the nineteenth century often depicted wealthy industrialists as overweight with money spilling out of their clothes. These successful capitalists were referred to as "Robber Barons" in the press. Even then liberals hated successful entrepreneurs. I guess newspaper reporters were anti capitalism even then. Some things never change.

A number of years ago, a history professor I know taught for a semester in a very poor country. His family was with him and he lived in in the country, away from the major city. Near their home was a massage parlor, a real massage parlor, not a sex parlor. His wife often frequented the place and took her mother for a massage when she visited. It was a nice thing to do and they were really cheap. Near the end of the massage the proprietor took her aside and with a big smile, and whispered in her ear, "Your mother is so fat." She meant it as a compliment. The only fat people in really poor countries are rich people. Remember rich and poor are relative concepts. This is an important issue because obesity is a huge medical issue and it is the poor who are obese in the US. Poor people in the US don't eat too much. They eat the wrong things. Maybe we need a fat czar to regulate what poor kids eat. They could be fed at school or other places to be determined by ACORN. CHEC could be the acronym for a new ACORN administered program. It stands for Children's Healthy Eating Centers. The Director of CHEC would be an important political appointment. It would be a much better job than being appointed the death czar who will determine if grandpa gets prostate surgery. Imagine the directed learning or reeducation that could take place at these CHECs while the food was being passed out. You could do anything from developing little spies to turn in their parents if they don't recycle, to getting their parents to vote for the right candidate. Do you think I am making this up? You couldn't make it up. It is a page out of Mao's *Little Red Book*.

Government health care bureaucrats will not only be making your health decisions, they will be collecting your data. They will know your health history and have your financial records.

I do not know many examples of what government does better that the private sector, but it is a lesson many people don't seem to understand. Friendly readers of drafts of earlier versions of this manuscript have suggested that government does municipal water systems, drug safety, bank regulation, and regulation of professions better than the market. I am not convinced. Government did not do well with flu vaccines and CPAs seem to regulate themselves pretty well. It seems so easy to see, but hard to understand. In the 90s, the government took over the Mustang Ranch whore house in Nevada. The law required that the government run Mustang Ranch when it was seized for tax evasion. They failed, and the Ranch was closed. The Nevada state government could not make money selling whisky and pussy in Nevada. Maybe some patrons worried about their record keeping, or maybe the product's quality just deteriorated. I just know it closed. I hope someone asks Harry Reid about this at his next town hall meeting.

Political Players and Things You Could Not Make Up

Charles Rangel is the best argument for term limitation I have ever heard or seen. A major problem with long serving elected officials is that they begin to believe they are "entitled." The most amazing thing about "stealing Charlie" is that he really, I mean really doesn't think he did anything out of the ordinary. And the sad thing is, if we knew the whole truth, he probably didn't. Rangel has spent 40 years in Congress and he insists that he is not guilty of any crime, maybe so if we ignore such things as pesky taxes on quasi illegal "gifts." Rangel's "friends" recently threw an 80th birthday party for him at the Plaza Hotel in New York City. He has no shame and neither do the party sponsors and I would add those who attended. That same week Dan Rostenkowski died. He was the Chairman of the powerful Ways and Means Committee in the House. In 1996, he was sentenced to17 months in prison for mail fraud. He was from Chicago. I would say there is something in the water in Chicago, but the entitlement disease is not limited to Chicago. It seems more like it must be in the water on Capitol Hill. When I read that Senator Ted Stevens of Alaska died, it brought yet another case to mind. Senator Stevens had a long and distinguished career and many Alaskans considered him the "father" of Alaska statehood. At the end, he too was brought down by entitlement disease. Consider this hypothesis for a working theory. The longer you serve the more powerful you become, the more likely you will become infected. If you are from Chicago the likelihood doubles. Chicago is so corrupt a jury couldn't convict Blago. They thought he was just doing normal political business.

As I was reading about Congressman Rangel I heard White House Press Secretary Robert Gibbs defending Michelle Obama's vacation, with daughter Sasha, in Marbella, Spain. He displayed annoyance about the question and dismissively commented that it was just a private citizen on a trip with her daughter. I hope he gets paid a lot for making such stupid statements for the entire world to hear. She is not a private citizen on a trip with her daughter. It is not only not private, we are paying for it. The room rates are over the top and unlike private citizens she is not paying for her stay and the stay of the presidential entourage. The Secret Service has to be there in force. There are 70 of them at about $1,400 per day. And then there is the little matter of air fare. It cost taxpayers about $178,000 to fly Michelle and Sasha to Spain. They will reimburse the government for the cost of two first class tickets to Spain. That will come to about $14,800. That means "WE" got charged about $163,200 to get them there and back. It struck me that this was not much different than the Rangel "issue," and it is disingenuous for the press secretary to claim it is a private citizen on a trip with her daughter. The trip was an official function that turned into a family vacation. Most importantly it is very expensive and it is being paid for by taxpayers. Today I saw the First Lady saying that the daughters were being raised like normal kids. I don't know any "normal kids" that have gone on such an expensive trip on taxpayer money. Most of us get reimbursed for business travel, not admitted vacation travel. I wonder if they will pay income tax on the $163,200 of our part of the trip. If they don't it is hard for me to see any difference between this and some of Congressman Rangel's issues. Maybe that is why he looks so surprised that anyone thinks he did anything wrong.

But let's be fair. Other First Ladies have traveled at our expense. As I remember, it was mostly with their husbands and mostly to their home base in Georgia, The Western White House, Kennebunkport, or "The Ranch." This is quite different and presents fewer challenges for the Secret Service. The First Lady's and First Daughter's trip to Spain is very different and reflects an attitude that they think they "own" government. Maybe the First Lady is working on a book of her own—maybe it even has a working title, something like The Audacity of Hope: Part II. Then the First Family went to Hawaii for Christmas. Same cost, same story. What the hell is wrong with Camp David? I looked up Audacity in my always handy American College Dictionary. Bingo! The 2nd definition is "bold in wrongdoing, imprudent and presumptuous." Now I get it.

Then along comes Congresswoman Maxine Waters. Representative Waters "represents" California. Come on, all she did was get political help for a bank in which her husband had a $250K of stock. And the head of the bank held a fund raiser for her in his home. And, oh ya, her chief of staff, Mikael Moore, was actively engaged in helping the bank. Mikael is her grandson. Money and nepotism are always an interesting combination. Come to think of it, US Congress is family business for Ms. Waters. The Congresswoman's lawyer called the allegations "exceedingly general." Hard to believe when her party is in charge. They must have been embarrassed. Representative Waters insisted, "I won't cut a deal." We have to wait this one out. My guess is she will cut a deal; she is the consummate deal cutter.

Charlie, Michelle, and Maxine think they have it coming. They are entitled. They "own" government. We should not be surprised; entitlement is what "community organizing" is all about. I don't think Thomas Jefferson, or Mr. Jefferson as he was referred to at UVA in the 1970s, had this in mind. Too bad he didn't think about term limits when he was setting this all up. He would have surely written it in.

Senator Byrd

Senator Byrd of West Virginia died in July, 2010. He was the longest serving Senator in US history and a great example of the need for term limits. The wooden catafalque that held his casket was the one built to hold Abraham Lincoln's coffin. I would bet Honest Abe was spinning in his grave. When Byrd was first elected to the Senate, he stood opposed to everything Lincoln represented. When he died he was the King of Pork. Now that is a political maturation if there ever was one. Earlier this year I saw a bumper sticker on a West Virginia car that said "Reelect Nobody."

Mark Dayton

Mark Dayton was recently elected Governor in Minnesota. In a political ad aimed at public school teachers, he identified himself as a former public school teacher. Come on, Governor, you grew up a rich, no very rich, exceedingly rich. You were born with a platinum spoon in your mouth. You cannot comprehend what it is to be a public school teacher. Voters, have you ever heard of Dayton's, as in the Dayton's stores. It's kind of like Caroline Kennedy working for a magazine.

Election Control

Watching TV coverage in Kuwait, I thought it was great to see the progress that had taken place, producing seemingly relatively safe elections. These changes may be permanent. Each voter had to "dunk" his or her finger into thick purple 24 hour ink. This was to make sure each person voted only once. That caused me to think we should adopt the same procedure. If the local election boards had done this in Minnesota last go around, Norm Coleman would still be in the Senate and Republican poll watchers would have a pretty accurate count of voters who tried to vote more than once for Al Franken. Actually, the Franken election count was even worse than people voting more than once. Minnesota law allows individual districts to interpret which votes are valid. Voters are asked to fill in an oval. However, some districts interpreted votes that did not fill in the oval. It was even reported that some votes for M. Mouse were accepted as Franken votes. Maybe Jimmy Carter should come to Minnesota to observe the next election, instead of going to some shit-hole, third-world election.

It struck me that we might follow historical tradition of "Landslide Lyndon," and forever refer to Minnesota's junior Senator as "Landslide Franken." LBJ got this moniker in his first race for the US Senate. He won by 87 votes in a recount. In the recount, 200 previously uncounted votes were "found" by Louis Salas the enforcer of George Parr, the "Valley's" political boss. All 200 votes were signed into the voting register in Alice, Texas in the same pen and the same handwriting two days after the polls closed. Abe Fortes won a federal district court decision preventing the Feds from intervening in the election recount because the election count was a states' rights issue (See Robert Carro, *The Path to Power*, 1982). I wonder how Abe got paid off by President Johnson. How about the Supremes? I find this particularly interesting as it shows clearly the beginning of LBJ from states' rights Texas politician to liberal big spending President, even more liberal than Kennedy, much more liberal. Ya just never know. It seems to me to define irony, it should be an example in the dictionary.

Giving Money to Charity

One thing that came out in the last election is that the conservative candidates for President gave more to charity than liberal candidates. Most notable, Republican candidate Mike Huckabee gave almost twenty percent of his income to a range of charitable causes. In contrast, the poster boy of chintzyness was Vice President Joe Biden. When Biden was a liberal Senator, he wanted to redistribute a lot more income to the poor. He wants to give your money to the poor, not his. The numbers on giving are startling. In May 2008, a Gallop poll asked people about their charitable giving and their political beliefs. The poll results were: very conservative gave 4.5% to charity; conservatives 3%; liberals 1.5%; and finally very liberal folks 1.2%. Conservatives also appear to not decrease their contributions in a recession as much as Liberals (*The Wall*

Street Journal, February 2, 2009). This is just more evidence that many liberals want to give your money to the poor, not theirs.

Tax Cheaters

Are Treasury Secretary Timothy Geitner, and the first nominee to be Health and Human Resources Secretary, Tom Daschle, so unique that President Obama couldn't find an honest taxpaying Democrat to fill the positions? That is either a condemnation of the abilities of the candidate pool, or an admission that there are a lot more tax cheaters among Washington types than we ever imagined.

Have you noticed that Geitner doesn't look people in the eye when he talks to them? I have never seen him looking into the camera or into the eyes of a person with whom he is speaking. When I was kid that meant you were lying. Daschle eventually withdrew. But not until it was reported that he had the use of a limousine supplied by a medical-related company under the regulation of Health and Human Services. President Obama had announced that he would have no people in his administration who had been lobbyists. Daschle was paid millions of dollars by a law firm where he worked with the health industry. I may be wrong, but I think that is the description of a lobbyist. Daschle did not withdraw his name until a *New York Times* editorial called for him to withdraw his name. I guess it is back to that high paying law firm lobbyist job. I bet he will not go back home to South Dakota.

Tax Promises Up in Smoke?

On April Fool's Day 2009, the federal tax on cigarettes went from 39 cents to $1.03, a 164% increase. During the campaign, President Obama said emphatically, "I can make a firm pledge… Under my plan, no family making less than $250,000 a year will see any form of tax increase. Not your income tax, not your payroll tax, not your capital gains tax, not any of your taxes." The cigarette tax falls heavily on the poor. Most rich people don't smoke. Reid Cherlin, a White House spokesman, commented that this was a promise the President kept. The cigarette tax revenue is earmarked for children's health insurance. Translation: there are promises and promises. Liberals certainly like children more than old poor smokers. They will decide what is best for you.

Calling All Dick Taters

On a swing with the President through Latin America, Secretary of State Hillary Clinton apologized for all the sins of past administrations, presumably even her husband's administration. This high level hand-wringing was met by leaders with great enthusiasm. The President of the Dominican Republic effused that it took great courage for her to see the error of past ways. When asked if she would go so far as building bridges to such leaders as would-be commie Hugo Chavez of Venezuela, Secretary Clinton was quoted in *The New York Times* (April 18, 2009) as saying, "Let's put ideology aside; that is so yesterday." Maybe that is what FDR was thinking when he sold out Eastern Europe to the commies.

Speaking of ideology, will Chavez put his ideology aside and stop the attacks on markets and the middle class? Will the Castro brothers release from prison all those that express a different ideology than theirs? Get serious, Madam Secretary, ideology isn't so yesterday. It is today and most frightening, will be tomorrow.

Mormons

I have noticed some curious ads on TV. They are Mormon ads. Now I have admiration for the Mormon Church and most of what they do. One time I said to a Mormon PhD student at Arizona State Arizona that I found some of the teachings interesting. He was asking me about the economics of Joseph Smith as it has some early utopian socialist rhetoric in it. He thought I was saying that I was "interested." Big mistake! I finally had to be obnoxious to get rid of them. I meant I was "intellectually" interested. I am sure I am still on a list somewhere.

But what are they doing running ads in selected TV markets? The ads show them to be just like all of us. A black man comes on and talks about the "normal" things he does and then concludes by saying "who am I? I am Mormon." Same ad for a skateboarder. Same for a—you fill in the blank. I found this very curious. Mormons are not like most of the rest of us. That is very evident in Wisconsin and Minnesota. To begin with, they don't drink. They send young men out on bicycles in suits around the world. Oh, and they wear "the garment." I don't know anyone else that wears "hair shirts." So what are all these ads about? Cynical old me. What it means to me is that Romney is running for President and the church wants to help. They are teeing up the ball for him. That is fine with me. As you know, I have already been through the "Catholic Thing." JFK was the first President that went to confession; Romney will be the first with a hair shirt. Speaking of confession and Kennedy, the priest must have had some good stories to tell his colleagues.

9

Race and Conversations on Race

Race is a dangerous subject to dive into for any reason. But let me put my white, Swiss, German, (most likely) Jewish, American toe in the water. We Boomers have been the most important players in race issues. Boomers of all races from all parts of the US got involved in the civil rights movement, before there was an anti-Vietnam war movement.

Let me begin by establishing a few experiences that allow me to step into rather than jump into this discussion. A friend and early reader of this manuscript suggested in reading my first chapter that I should use the term African American when talking about my black fraternity brothers. I told her they were referred to as Blacks in 1963. This was not a derisive term. A few days later, I was reading an article about the history of the Chase Hotel in Walker, Minnesota. A neighbor of mine had recently renovated and updated the Chase and sent me a copy of an article on the old hotel that had appeared in *Minnesota History* (Summer 2009). In the article, the authors point out that the original owners hired a Negro chef. But they say, "In 1904, J.T. Love, an African American chef, was hired from Chicago." Come on. I am sure the historically correct term in 1904 was Negro, not Black, and surely not African American. And this is a publication of the Minnesota Historical Society. Such attempts at pseudo political correctness are aggravating. It demonstrates how much attention academics pay to what they perceive is the politically correct thing to say.

Some people even have an incentive to create turmoil over misunderstandings as they make a very good living once the turmoil erupts. You know who they are. They are usually first on the scene when any turmoil boils up. Hell, the most prominent even show up at important funerals in order to be seen on TV. They show up when it is hard to imagine the purpose of their showing up. I wonder how all of these great friends of Michael Jackson could have let his condition go on. Were they unaware that he was so dependent on drugs? It seems to me that one of two things has to be true. There either should be more people being charged by the police, or these same people should be more truthful about their relationship with the pop star. Maybe if more were investigated we would learn that they were "around" a lot less than they implied.

Ryan and Susan after a discussion on race with Reverend Jackson.

In 1992, I was President of the University of Texas at Arlington. I asked a number of long time administrators to retire from their administrative post. It was time for change. Indeed I was hired to be that change agent. We in academe usually joke that they are "returning to their first love, teaching." This is an academic inside joke as if it were a first love they could have done it on their own without a kick in the ass by a new administrator. It was clear to most folks that I was to make sweeping changes, but most of the existing administrators, many of them who had been candidates for the job, seemed surprised by it. Academics are slow to figure some things out. Mostly they don't understand bureaucracy even though they have worked in it most of their lives.

I then set out to hire a new university provost. After a lengthy national search, I hired an African American, which was the proper term 1992. In my view he was the best qualified candidate in the pool. His name was Dr. Dalmas Taylor. He had previously been Provost at the University of Vermont, a very high quality place. There was turmoil on campus and some of it was racially motivated. I received death threats. I had nigger lover (no quotation marks) painted on a cement donkey that was hung on the pipe fence outside my home. This scared Susan a great deal as she is an animal owner and lover and we had lots of animals. She thought it was one of our animals when she first saw it. Yes, that was in Texas in 1992. Three nights later, the gate to our house was chained and locked. The police had to cut the chain so we could get out. I wore a bullet proof vest to spring graduation at the insistence of the campus police and Texas Rangers. The two people standing closest to me for this commencement were university police officers with bullet proof vests under academic robes to match mine. Eventually, the University police installed a hidden camera in the trees by our gate. No one was supposed to know about the camera. The next day we were vandalized again and the camera was gone. Now that is a meaningful warning. Susan got her deer rifle out and kept it loaded on the mantle. A Texas Ranger and I don't mean a baseball player, told her not to have it out if she couldn't shoot an intruder. She assured him she could and would. He liked that.

During this period, I had many conversations about race, profiling, and related topics with Dalmas. We became friends. We skied together and partied together. Susan and I attended parties with him and other professional African Americans in the Dallas, Fort Worth area. At some of these parties, we were the only whites attending. Dalmas often made fun of my inability to dance. At these parties they referred to me as the white boy from Wisconsin with absolutely no rhythm. Is that a profile? Years earlier when I said, "might as well, can't dance," I meant it.

I learned a great deal from these discussions. Some shocked me. Others informed me. Sometimes we agreed. Other times we agreed to disagree. Sometimes I just kept quiet. On one such occasion, while Dalmas and his wife, Faye, were visiting us in Colorado, they told us with great passion, that they did not think O.J. was guilty. I told him that I had read an article by a psychologist. (Dalmas had a PhD in Psychology) In it, the psychologist argued that there was no jury in America with African American women on it that would convict a black professional man, particularly an athlete, of killing his attractive white wife. The article argued that the most pissed off groups in America were African American women and Asian American men. He went on to argue that significant numbers of white, professional, successful men marry Asian American women and significant numbers of rich African American men, particularly athletes, marry white women. In both cases, these are very good looking women. So the Asian men and the African American women are pissed off about losing these potential mates. In fact, so pissed off they think the women have it coming. Or, as we said in the 1950s, it's "just desserts." Dalmas did not like this argument, so, on this issue I just kept quiet.

We talked about profiling. I argued with him that sometimes profiling is wise, learned behavior. It is the use of meaningful statistics. I related to him that when I worked at the US Treasury, I lived in Georgetown and walked about twenty blocks to work. I worked into the evening about one night a week. When I walked home, I was alert. If I saw a group of teenage Blacks coming toward me on the street, I crossed to the other side. Was I profiling or was I just being smart? At this time, as now, a startlingly high percentage of the teenage Black population in central cities were somewhere in the criminal justice system. My guess is that this is still the case. Even now when I am in Fort Worth and I am walking my dog at night, I avoid all young men of all colors. When I was a kid, I profiled the electric range. When the burners were orange, I avoided touching them. My wife, who is often in "the moment," was advised by her internist to be alert to her environment. That may be a much more politically correct way of expressing the same point.

Having "teed up" the race ball, let me say that I think President Obama really stepped in it when he weighed in on the arrest of Professor Henry Lewis Gates, Jr. More importantly, I don't think his comments were unplanned. He intended to say what he said. His profession before he entered elective politics was as a community organizer. This sort of racial confrontation is the language of community organizers. I was amused to hear President Obama characterize the protests at the health care town hall meetings as being organized, as if this depreciated their importance.

Sergeant James M. Crowley, the cop at the center of Professor Lewis Gates, Jr. controversy did not strike me as a racist. Many jokes circulated around academe that all had the same theme and centered on if Crowley was guilty of any profiling, it was profiling arrogant Harvard professors ranting "Do you know who I am?" Even the woman who called 911 came under scrutiny.

All she did was report two people breaking in, using the best description she was able to give. She then was asked if either was Black or Hispanic by the 911 dispatcher. She responded that "one of them might be Hispanic." This was not correct, but, more importantly it was also not a racist statement. She was answering a direct question from the 911 operator. Nine months later the Police reported in their "investigation" into the controversy that police officer Crowley "missed opportunities to find a better outcome" and that Professor Gates should have followed the police officer's (that would be Sergeant Crowley) requests. I wonder if it will be in the news when Sergeant Crowley takes "early" retirement.

Let's go back to my experience as a university president. I was under a lot of fire. Some of it was for the changes I had been hired to make. Some of it was for hiring Dalmas. I was asked to come to a meeting in Dallas. The "hosts" for this meeting were a very prominent African American minister who was the one African American on the Board of Regents of the University of Texas System (in those days they only had one) and a local African American community organizer, Darren Reagan. He led a protest over my hiring as there had not been an African American on the search committee. He often wore mirrored sun glasses and frequently got right in my face over sometimes exaggerated, racial issue, or even contrived problems on campus. He started the meeting by saying that when I arrived on campus he hated me, but he had decided that I was an honest, fair player. There were about twenty five African American men in the room. I was the only white. The meeting ended with the statement that they were "going to shut the campus down to protect my job." They said they were going to ask Jessie Jackson to come to Texas and "run" the protest. Earlier that same month a white Republican State Senator screamed at me in a public forum using extreme, "colorful" (as in racial), expletives that he was not going to "let his University become a protest movement." Yes, he was screaming. I resigned the day after this meeting.

As an aside, I should point out that being a community organizer can be a lucrative career. A few of the community organizers I knew as a university president did quite well on the income side. Some of them are now in jail and others are under indictment. It is not a career without risks. I would say some of the ACORN organizers are a case in point.

Now the lesson that President Obama takes from Harvard Gate is that it was a teaching moment. Consider an earlier Obama Administration teaching moment on race. Before Harvard Gate, Attorney General Eric Holder called for a National Conversation on Race. Shortly thereafter, and in unrelated chronological order, in different parts of the country, a chimpanzee in California attacked a woman (who now has a new face) visiting the chimpanzee's owner. The police shot the chimp. Shortly after that, *The New York Post* published a political cartoon of cops killing a chimp, who was the author of the Obama bailout plan. I chuckled when I saw the cartoon because I did not like the plan and thought it was very poorly conceived. This cartoon was quickly subject to racist accusation by none other than Attorney General Eric Holder. I thought the cartoonist was saying that it was written by a chimp. I certainly did not think the cartoonist was implying that the President wrote the plan. Not the President. Not only did he not write it, I am sure he did not read it. He does not have the time. He is too busy traveling. All Presidents rely on their economic advisors to write these plans and later brief them on the contents so they can sound like they understand it. If anything, the cartoonist had to be implying that Tim Geitner was a chimpanzee. And that would even be wrong. Tim Geitner likely only led the team that wrote the plan. He may have had time to read it, but I doubt it. The bottom line is that the Attorney General's complaint forced the *Post*'s owner, Robert Murdock, to apologize for the cartoon. In his apology, he said that "the *Post* will work to be more sensitive" (*Star Tribune*, February 25, 2009, p. A10). That ended any national conversation on race. The lesson I learned from the Attorney General's teaching moment, is when you're pissed about anything and are an African American, it's a good strategy to play the race card. Later, Glenn Beck said he thought the President was a racist for bringing this whole incident up. They sure taught him a lesson, a very quick lesson. He spent the next week back tracking on his show on Fox. They got to his advertisers.

A former head of the Civil Rights Commission, Mary Francis Berry, has acknowledged that President Obama uses race to polarize Americans and divert attention away from other problems. She stated that, "The charge of racism is proving to be an effective strategy for Democrats because having one's opponent rebut charges of racism is far better than discussing joblessness." I guess it is always a good strategy to change the subject when you are caught.

10

The Media

It makes me sad that newspapers are soon going to be extinct. It makes me sad, but, "like I totally" get it. I am sorry, but I just chatted with a neighbor kid and they all talk alike because it is infectious, maybe more so than H1N1. The extinction of the city newspaper makes me almost grieve because nothing makes me more content than to get up early, very early and have some strong coffee which my wife makes at home. And sit in a comfortable chair, leaning back, way back, and reading the local news, the national news, and sports, in that order. The better the sport pages, the better the paper: box scores, betting lines, etc., etc., etc. I reserve the sports pages until the end, for the same reason that my grandfather saved the small front triangle of a piece of pie for the end. He thought it was the best so he wanted to save it.

What makes me so sad is that print news just took a Kevorkian. The demise of print news is mostly a self inflicted demise. They forgot their market and they unionized every aspect of their operation. It is a tale much like the US Auto industry. What makes it different is that it is a national phenomenon rather than a Michigan issue. There will be a lot of hand wringing. Typical is Peter Kann a Pulitzer Prize—winning reporter and past chairman of Dow Jones and Company. "The decline of newspapers is a tragedy for democracy. How can it be stopped?" (Peter R. Kann, *The Wall Street Journal*, September 26, 2009).

I call a big BS on these kinds of statements. High union driven costs and liberal drivel did the papers in. It was for sure accelerated by changing technology. But it can no way be called a tragedy for democracy. Come on. The first reason it is not a tragedy is that there are many alternative sources of news today. The internet has made the news more accessible, everywhere. It has freed the news. Would be dictators on the right and left had to take over the radio stations and newspapers in bygone years. Now they have to control the internet. And even the Chinese have difficulty doing this. The computer geeks in every country in the world know what is going on in real time. This is a blessing for democracy. Let the liberals hand wring over the death of print journalism. It is mostly a problem for those who are in control of the print media. It is a tragedy for the families of these folks, just like it always is for those invested in old technologies, when new technologies are invented. Technology means we will have plenty of sources of news. Indeed, technology makes it almost impossible for totalitarian regimes to control the news. Keep in mind that many folks don't like freedom of speech. Even folks who should know better. The White House and we all know who that means, has even taken to attacking Fox News as not being the real news like ABC, NBC, and CBS. The only problem with these attacks is that they are serious and that is scary, yes even Nixonesque. Look for an Obama enemies list. Most of us are smart enough to determine who is giving us real news. We don't need White House spokespeople to tell us.

I live in two places, in the circulation area of *The Minneapolis Star Tribune* and of *The Fort Worth Star Telegram*. Both have a good sports section. In Minnesota, I am often, too often, disappointed because my paper is not there in the early morning. So often I will soon decide it is not worth the disappointment. If my mail came earlier I would subscribe to *USA Today*, mostly for their sports. I do get *The Wall Street Journal* in the mail, but usually not until late afternoon. With *The Wall Street Journal*, which we call "the Wall", late delivery is not as significant an issue. I used to buy *The Star Telegram* at a corner paper dispenser so I didn't encounter the disappointment of no paper.

Locals call *The Star Telegram* in Fort Worth the "Startle-Gram," and in my part of Minnesota, *The Star Tribune* is referred to as the "Red Star." Here in lies a major problem in daily print news. It is sensational and worse, has moved very far left from their readership. Reporters are the product of left-liberal schools of journalism, and editorial writers are mostly pretty far left of center. Add the fact that many are heavily unionized and you not only get left liberal spewing, but this spewing has high production costs. I suspect they would have gone out of business much earlier if it weren't for the sports angle. The irony is that the lefty reporters and editorialists look down their noses at the sports writers, who have been their meal ticket for a least a decade, if not longer. That is easy to understand. They look down on everyone, even their readers, the customers.

Demand is decreasing for the print media for two major reasons. Younger people find it much more convenient to get their news on the internet. They are accustomed to leaning forward to read. Also they don't drink coffee at home. The first is a technological advance that decreases the demand for a daily newspaper. This is the equivalent of imported cars in the auto industry. The coffee effect is a social change. Young people drink their coffee out. They also discuss their coffee orders at length. Then the papers themselves have been increasing their prices and this decreases the quantity demanded. For years I have purchased The *Fort Worth Star Telegram in* the morning for 50 cents from the dispenser. Recently the price was raised to $1.00. The reason that was given was that the paper had financial problems and needed revenue. Fathom that. A 100% increase in one day. I stopped buying it. I guess this shows that not many economists work in the city newspaper industry. The last advice economists would give a paper facing a declining demand is to increase price. I guess next they will be asking for a federal subsidy to stay in business. They might argue that it makes as much sense as aid to Chrysler and health care, maybe more. You could drive to the hospital in your subsidized Ford, sit in the governmental waiting room at the federal hospital, and read the government newspaper. It's sounding to be a lot like a social democracy. I fear for our children, no, your grandchildren.

The Wall Street Journal seems to be adding more sports every day, more pages of sports, box scores, and betting lines, even color pictures. Very soon there will be no need for a Boomer to get the local pinko rag. We have all moved around so much we are interested in national sports news rather than local team hype. Come to think of it, I am going to cancel today. They will continue to go out of business and they will wring their hands and say technology did them in. I would argue technology and ideology—and not even subtle ideology did them in. Serves them right, pun intended.

The *Wall* has learned fast. It has more sports each month and has recently added a magazine named *The Magazine from The Wall Street Journal.* It is a slick "Esquire"ish quarterly that comes with the normal subscription to the paper. These folks have come a long way with new ownership. It proves that it makes a difference if folks who know something about business run the business of producing newspapers. I have felt for some time that if the *Wall Street Journal* added a two page section a la the *USA Today* that gave a "snapshot" of an important news story from each state and each big city, it would render all other print news redundant. I offer that advice free to *The Wall Street Journal*! The state blurbs are important because we Boomers have moved around so much we have more than the normal number of "reference" places, and it amuses and entertains us to think we are checking in.

Television

Some of the same problems that infect print journalism can be found on network news. It is very left liberal, but faces competition from the internet and Fox News. The liberal press and politicians attack Fox as being biased. If you know any history, this is predictable, but still frightening. Some of the same issues are in play here, but it is a more swiftly moving trend.

Letterman joked on TV, after his recent sexual harassment issues, that he heard he is being impeached. For those who care about these sexual things, the economic equivalent of impeachment is just turning off the CBS channel. It might also be mentioned that every, I repeat every, private and public institution in America has rules against what we might call Clinton/Letterman behavior. I really don't care how consenting adults carry on, even under their desk. But, be assured if the junior accounting clerk on the 3rd floor were accused of this behavior, their cheating ass would be out the door. Where have all the feminists gone. "Oh, Ya –Ya," as they say in Minnesota, there are rules and there are rules. I was always confused by that argument.

The network news oriented shows are going to face many of the same problems that plague print journalism. They are going to face increasing competition from internet based programming. They have already tried to incorporate technology into their programming. The local NBC affiliate in the DFW area always asks a morning question and viewers can text their response to Channel 5, about what they think about something. The NBC affiliate in MSP recently asked viewers to text them their morning routine. The very next day they reported that John T. has a bagel with cream cheese and coffee, every day. Riveting viewing. Do you think that is the most interesting response they received? I guess their research shows this causes viewership to increase. What amazes me is how many respond. Maybe it is a measure of the vacuous nature of viewers. I guess it is a way for the station to get the public to buy into the show. They can tell each other how they feel about something. I find this a colossal waste of time. I would rather see an interview with someone who knows something. I don't want to waste my time hearing the opinion of someone who has so little to do they text a station about how they feel about something. Sometimes these "issues" are very trivial. I for one thing don't care much about how people feel except for when the polls close on an election night. I often have students who want to talk to me about what they feel about something. I direct them to a member of the clergy and I tell them I don't give a shit about what they feel, but I would be happy to talk to them about what they think. The amazing thing is that they don't get the difference. I blame this on the schools.

The networks have also taken over control of your volume dial. They increase the volume of the program for important things, like teasers and commercials. It is driving me to listen to Sirius. I can listen to what I want at the sound level I choose. I suppose we will all be forced to buy new TVs that control their own volume. Maybe this is a federal plot to stimulate the TV industry. Probably not. Even the Feds know that would be a stimulus to production in other countries, as very few TVs are produced in the US.

Let's look at the network news. Here we really have three components. The morning show that is the show in the morning. They usually come on at the local level at 5 am and focus on the weather, big headline events, and the rush hour traffic. We watch it for the weather and ignore the traffic as we have the luxury of avoiding rush hour. Then comes morning network shows at 7 am. These have shifted away from hard news and are mostly attempts at being entertaining. These reporters go out of the way to promote the idea that they are your friends. During the day, the network affiliates will interrupt scheduled programming at any time to tune into the day's police chase, looting, bombing, or staged hoax. All the networks and even the local news refer to criminals, using terms like, "that gentleman." Hey guys they are pukes, not gentlemen. Are they worried about offending them? But let's look at network peculiarities.

NBC

As I have aged, I have come to find much of what I see on NBC is boring or even worse. The "Today Show" seems to sink to new lows every day. My wife likes the show because it is familiar, so it drones on while I drink my coffee and read the newspaper, leaning back.

Today on "Today," no last week, or is it next week, the "NBC Today Show" had/will have a young boy with his father and mother on their morning show. The father had taped the boy returning home from dental surgery and it was a sad thing to watch. It focused on the young boy coming out of the anesthetic. The boy spoke a lot of nonsense and some fear. The father taped it and put it on YouTube. The father had come under criticism from *The Chicago Sun Times* for recording his son and then even worse, trying to make him a celebrity. But the father and mother, looking like candidates for Jenny Craig, saw it as way to further compound the foolishness by getting on national TV. Matt asked him if he thought his son would be embarrassed in the future. He replied "no worse than the pictures my mother took of me." Shame on him. His mother put them in a scrapbook that is now most likely moldy in the attic. He put his son on YouTube. But let me call a bigger shame on NBC. They put it on national television and played it at least twice. I wonder at what point the networks will stop the escalation of nonsensical trash. Maybe when we turn it off. And all the while, Al Roker is cackling in the background.

If you are asked to go on the "Today Show," don't. I am amazed at the people who go on for their 30 seconds of fame. Just recently there was a 45ish looking couple with their teenage daughter who had some problem with the cheerleading coach. She quit the team and they went after the coach, who it turns out had posed for Playboy before she took the coaching job. The high school fired her and other parents wanted her hired back etc., etc., etc. It seemed to me, half listening, that they wanted her fired and that they had some difficulty understanding the grievance against this Playboy posing cheerleading coach. It struck me as pathetically funny. From what I have observed in the kids of friends and family, teenagers are actively sending nude pictures of themselves to friends and acquaintances, some even to workmen that traipse through the house on some repair mission. What these kids don't understand is that these pictures may well bite them in the ass when they become a cheerleading coach or a brain surgeon. Many of the people appear to need counseling—or at least therapy—get a life. If you are asked to appear—tell them you'll call back in the morning. I promise, you really will look like fools. And all the while Al Roker will be cackling in the background.

Where in the world is Matt Lauer? I must confess, I could give a shit where Matt Lauer is, ever. In many ways, watching "The Today Show" chronicles the lowering of American cultural standards. But I guess I should be more careful about this. About the time TV was first coming into my Boomer consciousness in the mid 1950s, "The Today Show" featured J. Fred Muggs, the morning TV chimp. He was a side kick of Dave Garraway, the first coming of Matt Lauer. Fred was a paid co-host. He ultimately got fired for biting the comedienne Martha Ray in 1957. Remind me, why was Martha Ray funny? My guess is that she had it coming. It was reported that Dave Garraway disliked J. Fred and that he spiked his OJ with Benzedrine to make him meaner, hoping he could get him off the show. Could you make this up? Shame on Dave.

The commies even got into the act of criticizing Mugs and NBC. *Izvestia* reported that J. Fred Muggs was necessary "in order that the average American should not look into reports on rising taxes and decreasing pay." You could not make this up. They had it half right; the first half.

Mugs even painted with oils on TV. Matt, Meredith, Anne and Al followed in J. Fred's footsteps recently and took lessons painting oil paintings of nudes. They then auctioned them off for charity. They displayed them so viewers could determine bids. They taped over the nipples. I promise I am not making this up. Actually, I remember J. Fred's paintings as better than Ann's.

TV Words

Some very useful words have been rendered absolutely meaningless by modern day television. "Exclusive report" means only that when they were talking to our station or network, they were not talking to others at the same time. In other words, it was not a News Conference, the "newsmaker," perhaps wannabee newsmaker was having a series of conversations with the media. We should start using the phrase "serial news conferences" like serial killers. In fact, sometimes serial wife killers do serial news conferences. Maybe we could petition Congress to outlaw the phrase "Exclusive Report." This might be an issue that Nancy Pelosi could put her (short) arms around. But why don't networks just stop talking to these pukes—it's like, ya know, they are all trying to be a version of *The National Enquirer.*

Another interesting phenomenon is the amount of thanks the reporters get for just doing their job. Matt is out covering some story, the case that comes to mind is the young man who cut his arm off when he got stuck in his basement. It really got a lot of "exclusive" air time on "The Today Show." About the sixth time I heard an exclusive story from Matt it went back to Al. "What an amazing story, thanks Matt." What is amazing to me is that I have worked for over 40 years in many different settings. I have never been thanked for doing my job. In fact I never expected it. I was getting paid for it. I guess the "Today" show folks don't get paid well for doing their job so the network insists they be thanked on air. Does Al get a cackling bonus? Thanks Al.

Today, "Today" was exclusively interviewing Dina Lohan during my coffee and newspaper. Dina Lohan, is Lindsay's mother. She was trying to provide cover for her pathetic, uninteresting daughter. Even Matt got testy with her because the bottom line is that she was blaming the judge for Lindsay being incarcerated. It was one of the best examples of home economics moral hazard that I have seen in a while. It is actually a good argument for the court taking 24 year adults "away" from their enabling parents. But, then I guess she is just defending her own meal ticket. I then Googled Lindsay Lohan. Guess what. Dina had given the same "exclusive interview" to other outlets. Serial exclusiveness.

I really chuckled when I saw that Richard Hatch, the first winner on "Survivor", was sent back to prison. You remember "big Dick." Not only was he the first winner, but he walked around nude on the show and he was very loud about his homosexuality. He went to jail for not paying taxes on his winnings from the show. He claimed the novel defense that he was being persecuted because he was a homosexual. Actually, the Feds care more about taxes than sexual preference. Anyway, big Dick was out of jail on house arrest, staying with his sister. He received a get out of house arrest card for an exclusive interview with Matt on Today. Later that day he was sent back to prison for violating his parole. He claims it was more "homo-persecution." I think the judge looked up "exclusive interview" in Webster's and saw it meant one. It turns out Dick had three exclusive interviews that morning and he was only approved for one exclusive interview. The judge would make my high school English teachers happy. Justice and good English. Bravo! And shame on NBC and Matt. First, bad taste, most of us would like to forget about Dick as we pay our taxes. Second, maybe more people should go to jail for multiple exclusive interviews. Or better maybe we will stop the use of the word exclusive.

Even worse is the tag, "A Report That You Will Hear Only on Channel 5." That is a big lie. It may well have already been on one of the others. If it is really news it will be on most of them in 10 seconds.

CBS

Katie Curic moved from early morning entertainment of NBC to the stately "CBS Evening News." Some of the competing "talking heads" at that time sniped that "she does not have enough gravitas for the job." I had to look it up. Now I use it whenever I can. She was in Kuwait and asked a sniper, "What do you feel when you are out doing your job, sniping?" He replied, "slight recoil." I laughed out loud. The "talking heads" were right.

I like "60 Minutes." For a long time I was curious about why. After the death of Don Hewitt it became clear where the quality came from. He was even able to put a lid on loudmouth Mike Wallace, from time to time. In one retrospective on his life, he is shown putting a lid on Wallace and not putting on Wallace's contribution for the week on that particular Sunday's show. He is shown over and over telling the reporters to tell a story, tell a story. After I saw this I was even more convinced that the show will not be on the air in three years. Most of what they do is pretty shitty and without Hewitt to keep them focused, they will decline in being relevant.

Also on "60 Minutes" you found Andy Rooney. He died shortly after retiring. The news of his death caused me to feel kindly about him. He died with his "boots on," a good way to go out. My father and father in law thought he was very funny. I did not. It is the demographic "thing." And demographic changes dominant markets and marketing. I think Herb Stein's son, Ben will replace him. He is funny and he is the right demographic, a better word than age in this litigious world we live in. If he is unavailable, I would be happy to send some tapes.

11

Sports

Watching sports is an integral part of our male Boomer experience. Many Boomers played very physical sports, such as basketball, into their 50s. This resulted in many sports injuries that were not related to interscholastic or intercollegiate sports. It also produced many limping 50 and 60 year old men and a good source of income for orthopedic surgeons.

We are the first to really have a cornucopia of sports available to us on TV. This was not the case when we were kids. My first memory of sports on TV was really sports on the radio. My paternal grandfather listened to baseball whenever it was on the radio at night. He would sit in his chair and listen to the Milwaukee Braves on the radio. These were the Braves of the Spahn and Sain and pray for rain era. Baseball was the sport he played in farm country as a young man. I would imagine it was the only sport they had in the early 20th century in rural Wisconsin. They did have plenty of fields, oops, farm land, and they could likely afford a ball and maybe a few gloves. I was told that he was good, but we all know how these memories go. My observation was that he worked hard manual labor during the day and mostly dozed off next to the radio at night. But he seemed happy. Once he even took me to Milwaukee to see a Braves game. I caught a foul ball hit by the great Warren Spahn. I still have it.

His youngest son, my uncle Mark, is only about ten years older than I, and he was a rabid baseball fan, even keeping detailed official scoring notes while he also watched grandpa Ed snooze. I suspect he still follows baseball carefully and even enjoys the World Series. I don't even watch it. I only have one friend that pays any attention and the poor bastard is a Minnesota Twins fan. He is my wife's cousin, Mark, and a long suffering Twins fan. He calls the Twin's star Joe Mauer, Baby Jesus Mauer. My conclusion from all this is that boys follow the sports their fathers watched on television. Most Boomers I know are close to the sports they played in grade school and high school or imprinted in college. For most Boomers this is not baseball.

Baseball is in fact dying as a spectator sport for white and black

Americans. It is a huge Latin sport and I would expect that Major League Baseball will start to move south. There are several reasons for this. The first is that big city kids in the US have not played baseball for a long while. There are very few baseball fields and many basketball courts. The results of this should have been foreseen. The second reason is the inability of baseball to change.

Baseball is the only TV sport that does not have a clock. Even golf has a sort of clock. This produces games that go on endlessly. Some playoff games that start at night, in the West go on for more than six hours. Five hours is common. If your beloved and powerful, with no salary cap, Yankees are playing in the West at night the games will end the next day, even a school day. So much for developing the young base.

For these reasons the quality of "America's Pastime" is declining in America. Castro was likely correct when he recently said that Japan and Korea field the best teams in the world. I think that is the only correct statement I have ever heard come out of his tyrannical mouth. If you remember he used to give five hour speeches and this is his first correct statement. It was inevitable, like a monkey at a typewriter.

Fans like fairness and until recently there is no instant replay for the umpires to use in baseball. Its present use is very limited. Recent playoffs were tainted by several very bad calls in crucial games. Instant replay would have very possibly changed the outcome. When asked about replay, the Commish responded that he was opposed because it would slow down the game. But Commish, more time was wasted by the manager arguing the call, than it would have taken to have instant replay and a fair call. So much for America's pastime. It's funny, but for some reason Americans really like fairness, whatever that is. After the manager goes on a tirade and is kicked out of the game, the pitcher gets added time to loosen up. The TV fans go take a pee, and get another beer to find that the game has still not restarted. Yawn, I might as well go to bed. Let's get on with it. I was listening to Colin Cowherd on the radio the other day and he said baseball is the only sport you can watch on TV and you do not really need to watch. I guess that is a better way of saying what I was trying to say.

Sports on TV were limited, but expanding when we early Boomers were in college. In college, we only got two pro football games on TV, either the Packers or the Bears. Since about half of my fraternity brothers were from Wisconsin or Chicago, these games were big fraternity events, with animated disagreement, even a few fights, but fighting was discouraged. If a real fight was called for we laced up heavy boxing gloves. These fights didn't last long as it is very difficult for fraternity boys to swing heavy boxing gloves for very long.

Since there was no cable, if the games were not sold out, we were screwed. We never thought of petitioning Congress to stop these blackouts. My guess is politicians then would not have even responded to such stupid entities. Those were simpler times. Now politicians stick their noses into these issues at every turn. Some politicians, who claim they are anti big government politicians, stick their nose into such things as the BCS selections. It is laughable when the anti-public health care Congressman from Texas wants the government to look into BCS selection. Oh, I forgot, he has TCU fans who vote in his district. Let me take that back, if they spent more time on this, they wouldn't have as much time to screw with us on other economic issues.

The other fountainhead of our fandom is sports we played. Since I went to a small enrollment high school, I was able to play both football and basketball. Even though I was not very good, actually bad, it was a great experience. I learned about competing in life from this participation. Some of the coaches were good guys who taught us life skills. Many were, truthfully, a colossal pain in the ass. Life and death pep talks when you know you are not worth a shit, is hard to take seriously. Good life skills, like how to deal with assholes, oops, I mean coaches, were learned.

My sports viewing is focused on pro football and college basketball and football. Pro basketball holds no interest for me and I don't have any Boomer friends who care about pro basketball. We think it is a bunch of thugs beating up on each other. I know they aren't (all) felons, but they look and dress like felons. Most importantly, there is no finesse; no defense. Worse, if you go to a game, it is so loud it is uncomfortable. Loud music and fireworks inside a building is awful if you are older than thirteen.

I was pleased, but amused to see that the NBA Commissioner, David Stern, was quoted as saying that LeBron James was "entitled" to leave Cleveland. No shit, David, this is America, not the baseball league in Cuba. The choice between NYC and Miami was interesting in an economic sense. Think about it. He could buy a mansion on the beach for the money he will save in NYC taxes and New York state taxes and even have money left for some fancy wheels. Maybe all those fancy financial folks will follow suit and move to a lower tax state. Most of their work is on the phone or computer. Why live in a place where the city steals so much money? Even worse, no nothing protestors make it difficult to go and come from work.

To be sure, gambling plays a role in much of the Boomer interest in sports. The growth of fantasy football is amazing. For many Boomers, it is an activity that consumes hours of research and chat during the season. The research starts months before the first games. The college basketball tournament and bracketology is an amazing Boomer phenomenon, inspired in large part by gambling.

Let's Play Chase

Why is it that so many Boomers' children and grandchildren played soccer and why is it that college and professional soccer have not generated the interest that was predicted as a game in the US? For years, I have heard predictions that it was about to take off in the US. It most surely is the most popular world sport. The bracket selection for the World Cup is viewed with as much enthusiasm as the college basketball brackets in the US. There seems to be a few very important reasons why world football doesn't appeal to Boomer Americans.

For us Boomers, it appears to me that it is more an activity than a sport. It is like recess kick ball was when we were in grade school. We never had any inclination to watch kick ball teams on TV after TV was invented. Hey, I know there was no kick ball league to put on TV. That is the point. It was called football in other parts of the world. Now hordes of boys and girls play soccer. They can even play together on mixed sex teams. When I drive past playing fields in the early evening and on weekends there are many fields and many kids and parents waiting their turn. Once they get a little older, most of them quit. Why? The first reason is the kids themselves. It is an activity for kids and grandkids of Boomers. They outgrow it in part because no one really wins or loses. How can it be a sport if the players don't compete, they participate? What a quaint idea; the idea of sports developing competitive kids. Oh, I forgot we are not into competing, we are into cooperating. I think that "Building the Cooperative Society" is a major course of study in the elementary education degree programs at US Colleges of Education.

Several years ago, I was helping a former friend move. Truthfully, I was watching him move, giving moral support, and drinking a beer. He was moving several boxes of trophies into his youngest daughter's bedroom. She was about to enter high school. I said, "I didn't know Molly was an athlete." He said "She isn't. The trophies are for participation." Bingo! Soccer for kids isn't a sport, it's a cooperative activity. The trophy is like a merit badge. I don't watch things in which I participated in school. I like to watch things I played competitively, even though our teams were not very competitive. We lost one basketball game my senior year 78-14! I was our high point man with 3 points, 3 free throws. I was our center at 6 feet 2 inches. Our competition had the first 7 footer in Wisconsin high school basketball. I think we even laughed about it. It was the competition that made it fun. We mostly lost. I was not permanently scarred. It actually taught me lessons of trying to find something you could be good at, or maybe more correctly stated, less bad at. What a great concept. In economics we call it comparative advantage.

My friend Metz argues that there are even more reasons soccer, sorry football, has not taken hold in the US. He argues that Americans like two important things in sports viewing. First, they like to see scoring. Secondly, they like their violence on the playing field, not in the stands. I would add a third issue. Americans don't like to attend competitions that end in a tie. When I read the box scores from the World Cup tournament in the fall of 2009, I saw a national score that ended in nil-nil. God, I'm sorry I missed that exciting struggle. Did anyone leave the stadium loudly chanting, "we're number one!"

The 2010 World Cup seemed to generate a lot of interest in the young adult market, even in the US, but it doesn't seem to carry over after the Cup. A game at the National Sports Center in Blaine, Minnesota, between the NSC Minnesota Stars and the Puerto Rico Islanders shortly after the Cup ended, drew 872 fans. *The Minneapolis Star Tribune* reported that the reserved middle section was superfluous. The reporter noted the contrast to the World Cup when Brits Pub in Minneapolis turned folks away during a Cup game. Brits (English style pub) has a capacity of 2,130. I get it, they really didn't give a shit about soccer. They came to drink a beer bombarded by that irritating noise that was argued to be so popular. Here to is a simple explanation. You could get drunk in loud peace and not have to talk to your girlfriend.

My wife and I were eager to learn what we were missing so we tuned into the Women's World Cup game between the US and Japan in 2011. Susan mostly dozed. I noticed as the game wore on that the clock was running up. I did not know how long it would last and I found this led to my disinterest. I decided then that they should play the clock down. I will send them my suggestion. Next, the game ended in a tie and they determined the winner by a kick off between one player from each side. I found this disappointing. For the life of me, I still have not figured out why or how such an unsatisfactory end was dreamed up. It will be my last time to watch.

All this leads me to believe that World Football will never become popular in the US. Let me qualify that a bit. World Football will not become popular in the US until we become as socialized as the rest of the world. In cooperating societies, a nil-nil score may be the preferred outcome. Was it Lenin or Stalin that liked the term "cooperating societies?" Problem is they meant cooperating with them. If Obama wins a second term, it may be on its way to becoming a popular US sport. But for me, watching curling on TV is much more interesting than World Football. Someone wins. And the curlers all get drunk together after the match.

Hey, World Football isn't even popular where it's popular. South Africa built 6 state of the art stadiums for the 2010 World Cup. Now, they don't have many uses for them. The company slated to take over the leases pulled out. Soccer games in South Africa have been drawing very small crowds, in the 200-500 range. Now that goes down as a wonderful public "investment" for a poor country.

Welfare For Rich Guys (and Good Seats for Local Politicians)

The new Arlington Cowboys Stadium, I should say the Dallas Cowboy Stadium in Arlington, is a wonder. What a great deal for Jerry Jones. What a bad deal for taxpayers. It is a case study on how rich team owners hold up cities for their own wealth enhancement. In the case of the "Boss Hog Stadium," as a local sports wag refers to the new home of the Dallas Cowboys, it was a bit different. Usually the owner of the franchise threatens to leave town for a new environment if taxpayers don't pony up for a new facility. You can watch for that in Minneapolis where a "Boss Zygi Stadium" is in the discussion phase. Zygi is reported to be considering a move to LA if the folks in MSP don't get off the dime on the stadium issue. Ed Roski Jr. is even helping Zygi by building a Taj Mahal stadium near LA. Zygi doesn't even have to threaten, he is going to move. Minnesotans know Roski has his eyes on the Vikings. I wouldn't be surprised to see that Zigi invited Ed to a game and to show him off. That would speed the process up in Minnesota. It makes sense. I have already heard the drumbeat. "We built a new stadium for the Twins and the Gophers. The Gophers are awful and not getting better. If we don't build a stadium the Vikings will go to California and then those bastards will have the Vikings and the Lakers." The local "rumor" now is that the League will not "allow" the Vikings to move. The League thinks that it needs a team in Minnesota to spread out TV coverage and increase TV revenue.

Jerry Jones was not (quite) so crass. Everyone knew he was not going to leave DFW for another venue. Instead he created a Metro competition for the Boss Hog location. The local districts went into a frenzy putting competing packages together. And like most public projects, it was sold on how much business it would bring to the local community that was able to win the competition for the stadium. The competing localities hired economists to calculate multipliers and project revenues for the community. The problem with all these calculations is that they are calculated as if this "new" money wouldn't have been spent on other items. A local might have bought a new shirt or gone to Six Flags, but the expenditure is treated like new spending. What I am trying to say is that these multiplier studies are mostly fiction. Fiction produced by economists for local politicians to make arguments about how dopey locals will be better off if they tax themselves to build a monument for Boss Hogg or Boss Ziggi. The reported cost of the Boss Hog stadium was $1.2 billion that *Sports Illustrated* reported was paid by Jerry Jones and the "munificent taxpayers." *Sports Illustrated* got it correct.

Don't blame the economists. They are doing it because they get paid to do it. Blaming the economists for the fictional big dollar revenue projections is a lot like blaming your wife's settlement on divorce lawyers. Anyone who keeps their own billable hours is well paid. It's the incentive thing. It is always the incentive thing.

To make these public works projects even worse for taxpayers, many of these taxes are exported. This means that they are placed by increasing taxes on motel and hotel stays and rental car fees. This makes them taxes on people who are not those who voted them in. This is taxation without representation at its worst. Maybe fans and businessmen renting cars at DFW Airport should have a Boss Hog Tea Party. I LOL during the Super Bowl when the TV commentators referred to the "Stadium in Arlington" as the "House that Jerry Built."

Prior to the election, the Cowboys' black players were brought into the

Arlington African American community to campaign for the tax increase in the "hood." This is very effective, and I would add cynical politicking. Do you think any of these community organizers get paid off for organizing this "grass roots" efforts. I bet the ministers do!

These special sales taxes become costs of production for businesses renting cars and hotel stays. The idea is that they are being paid by fans, but this is fiction. There are only a few games per year. The taxes are passed on to consumers of the goods the taxed firms produce. Economists refer to this as the incidence of the tax. It is a good deal if you can get it. It is welfare for rich guys. I think most folks understand this and just don't give a shit. They want a team. This is the cost of democracy with uninformed voters. But still better than the alternative.

I started this section with a subtitle "and good seats for politicians." How and why? That is a good question. Who would you guess has a free (to them) luxury box in these public financed stadiums? Take a guess. The mayor and city council have a free luxury box with food and refreshments. Why? City development. Nice work if you can get it. The Arlington version of the Fort Worth paper recently reported on this box and a bit of a scandal arose. These same city council members were angered by the criticism. They just don't get it. It would be nice to see a guest list of who was "being developed." I wonder if any friends, relatives, kids, or political donors were part of the city development guests. The paper reported that the City Council would have to pay extra—a lot extra—to keep the City Council Box for the Super Bowl. A Council press release printed on the front page of the paper said the City Council declined to pay the extra amount. I guess "City Development" isn't done on Super Bowl Sundays.

The 2011 Super Bowl and all its inclement weather was fun to watch. We were in Fort Worth and live just a few blocks from Sundance Square, ground zero for ESPN. The coverage fueled the Arlington taxpaying fans feelings of rejection. They were "enraged" that the stadium was being "billed" as Jerry's Superdome. Some reporters even referred to it as the Super Bowl in Dallas, others, North Texas. One enraged taxpayer/fan wrote to *The Star Telegram*, "I'm paying for the stadium with my tax dollars, not anyone in Dallas." These same Arlington taxpayers who had been "duped" into building a stadium in Arlington for the Texas Rangers are a bit happier with the Rangers. They showed their "gratitude" to the taxpayers by naming their stadium the Ball Park in Arlington. It sits adjacent to Boss Hog Stadium. Believe it or not they "share" parking, which is a rare efficiency in the stadium business.

State Government also can't stay out of these sports "transfers." The State of Texas pitched in $31 million to "help" pay for the Super Bowl in Jerry's House. "They," whoever they is, argued that there was "good return" on this investment. I wonder how many good seats they got? I always cringe when I hear government officials use the term investment.

Levelland, Texas got a $3,000 "investment" for hosting the "little Dribblers Basketball Tournament," for boys. Again, women's sports gets screwed, no, again taxpayers got screwed.

This is the sports version of the government tit. These are transfers from all taxpayers to higher income folks. This is the state and local government version of earmarks. And I would bet the locals don't like earmarks and think the Bridge To Nowhere was a waste of tax money. Some of the folks in Levelland are likely Tea Party Members.

Women's Sports

Women's sports at the college level has grown by leaps and bounds over the years. An important question is, who watches them. The dirty little answer is that almost nobody watches them. Huge transfers of money take place in college athletic departments. The NCAA has become more interested in gender equity than competition. I once participated in an NCAA "Certification" visit to the University of Illinois. Each Certification team was composed of a university president, an athletic director, a faculty representative, and a "Senior Woman." The NCAA created the Senior Woman position to create equal opportunity for women in college sports administration. All NCAA Division I and II athletic programs were required to have a Senior Woman position. When we visited the U of Illinois campus, the Senior Woman on our visitation team measured the office of both the Men's and Women's BB head coach to determine if they were the same size and had the same furnishings. I promise I am not making this up. Later I chaired a trip to LSU. It turned out the Senior Woman at LSU was a black man. That did not go over very well with the Senior Woman on our visitation team. The AD argued that the NCAA required that schools create a Senior Woman's position, but they did not specify that it had to be filled with a woman. I had to step out in the hall to keep from laughing. Later I asked the black man who was the Senior Woman if he ever felt uncomfortable in the position. He answered that he was uncomfortable only when they went to meetings and the gifts he got were women's clothes and watches. I am not clever enough to make this up. I don't mean to embarrass anyone, but only to point out how ridiculous this bull shit is. The whole NCAA operation is driven by parity and gender equity.

In 50 years they will want all games to end with a tie score to avoid any hurt feelings. And you thought college sports was about competition. This is already part of kids' sports like T-ball in, of course, California. If one team gets too far ahead the game ends. And the team with the too high score loses. I am not making this up. My friend, Mark Seidl, who drew the cartoons for this book observed it first hand while visiting his grandson in, you guessed it, California.

Only some men's football and men's basketball programs pay for themselves. I mean paying for themselves in tickets sales, including gifts that determine seating priority. At Clemson, where I was Dean of Business they had a very successful athletic booster money raising operation called IPTAY. This originally was a group, I Pay Two Dollars a Year, thus IPTAY. In the 1980s when I was there, it meant more like "I Pay Thousands A Year." Lifetime giving determined everything, like seat locations, tickets to Bowl games, and tickets to the ACC Basketball Tournament, a very tough ticket to get. It is a well-run operation and semi-independent from the University. Some folks hate these operations, but if you are going to be competitive you better have one.

According to the NCAA, the average revenue for football was recently $1.95 million and for men's basketball was $.5 million in the 119 Division I schools. No other sports, men's or women's, make money. The biggest loser among major male sports is baseball, losing an average $.7 million. Average women's losses were not listed I guess some things are better if kept secret. The truth of women's collegiate sports is that they exist only because of a huge subsidy from taxpayers, students, and the "revenue sports." These revenue sports are big time college football and basketball, and maybe even hockey in the Mid-West and North-East. It is just part of the world that we live in. Some colleges have even added sports for women in an attempt, pushed by the NCAA, to have equal participation. Equal participation of women and men at any college is difficult because football squads are big. These new NCAA sports include rowing and equestrian events. This is an interesting transfer. It is a transfer from minority football and basketball players to rich white girls. Gymnastics as a women's collegiate sport doesn't work too well as the girls, I mean women, are too old to be good gymnasts. Their bodies are too woman like.

Recently a university tried to count cheerleaders as athletes to get their female athlete head count up. This claim was rejected by the NCAA. My bet is that it will soon be approved as the NCAA views equality as equal participation—that means the same number of male and female athletes. This is difficult to achieve if you play football because no women's sports require as many players per team as football. You do the numbers.

I don't know any people who attend women's collegiate sports to watch. I suspect that attendance is limited to friends and family. I read somewhere that Coach Wooden reported that he thought women's college basketball was the purest form of basketball being played today. I guess my friends are more into men's skills.

The Women's NBA is unique in that it is transfer in the private sector. The NBA subsidizes the Women's NBA and very few fans attend. You can see this for yourself. Tune into a game and you will notice that the cameras try to avoid scanning the stands. A friend of mine took his daughters to a Women's NBA game and he claimed that the fans were mostly black men and lesbian women. I have no idea how he determined this to be true. Let me be politically correct and point out that I don't care what the NBA owners and Players Association do with their revenue. I just find it curious. It doesn't exist in other areas. At least I have never heard of it. Does the Miss America pageant support a pageant for young men?

Sports and Drugs

It seems to me that baseball was more interesting when the players were "juiced up." It also seems to me that it was pretty clear who was doing it and who was not doing it. Hey, they looked different. They even looked different from themselves several years earlier. Along these lines, I was not a bit surprised when I read that Lance Armstrong and other cycling racers were doing performance enhancing drugs. They were doping. Now I am not a cycling fan, and I often forget what the French race is called, but I do tune in to watch it every summer. It always seems to me that you could not do this if you were not taking something.

I was recently grilling on my Texas condo's public grill, not a government public good, a local private public good, a "club" grill, and I met a new neighbor. We chatted and I found out he was a pro bike racer. I had just read about bike racing and drugs and I asked him about it. He replied that all racers "dope." It is always gratifying to find what I assumed to be true all along to be so. Then the real question is what Lance did to piss them off enough to break their silence. I guess he just got too good. Maybe he is an ass hole, most likely both. Those seem to me to be the only two explanations and both seem true.

The bottom line is that women and men who train hard to be athletes are adults. It seems to me that if they want to work out constantly, eat right, spend years in the weight room, practice mind numbing hours for a slim chance of success, it is their business. If you start banning one for doping, why not ban them for all performance enhancing activities. That might include lifting weights, going to college five years for four years of eligibility (that extra year is certainly performance enhancing) or leave college without a degree. These seems like distinctions without a difference to me. The point is that many athletes do many things that give them an advantage over other athletes. Isn't that what training is all about? This all seem like nit picking, and nit picking pisses most Boomers off. As we said as kids, "same difference."

Sports Do Gooders and Politics

Like banning performance drugs, some other do gooders want to ban trash talking fans. A Wisconsin high school has banned the use of "negative chants" such as "AIR-Ball" and "OVER RATED" at basketball games. Maybe these are mostly liberals that think they know what is best for you or maybe they just don't like sports because they don't like competition. Some colleges' faculty are seeking to ban fraternities and sororities because they are exclusive. Logically, country clubs will be next. Maybe these folks don't like sports and fraternities because they think they are development programs for Republicans. After all, they promote "competition." Maybe they will propose a special golf tax. It is elitist and competitive, and done in exclusive clubs.

After this year's World Series, some of these same do-gooder talking heads were blathering about the presence of cigars in the winning locker room. Yet, another reason to ban "outsiders" from the locker room. Logically, I suppose we should consider banning cigars from wedding receptions. Perhaps we already have.

Sports, Politics and Sportsmen

Speaking of sports as political development programs, most coaches vote Republican. Lou Holtz says the standard most coaches set for their players conforms to the GOP version of American society. Only one college football coach gave money to the Obama campaign.

My wife thinks Brett Favre is the ultimate prick tease. I agree with her, but I still like him, I am from Wisconsin, after all. He made sports pages more interesting when the only other Wisconsin professional sport was baseball. Most Baby Boomers are pleased when NFL training camps open.

John Daly drank almost the same thing as Arnold Palmer, lemonade and ice tea, but with vodka. That is an important difference, I think. It sounds better. How did Tiger Woods have time to practice? For years I wondered why fans screamed "get in the hole" when Tiger hits a drive. Now I know. I suspect Tiger will not recover as a pro golfer. My wife thinks this is just desserts.

Speaking of golf, I have trouble understanding the fascination that aging Boomers have for golf. They even play golf with their wives. Women shoot from different tees. They talk with their friends when you're shooting. I guess if you have a bad shot you have something to blame it on other than your prostate issues. Any man who claims to like golfing with women is lying. And as aging Boomers get even older, it will get worse. Consider again that even Arnold Palmer looked bad when he hit the opening drive at Augusta.

It is time to switch to bridge. You don't spill your gin. It is fun to do it with women It doesn't get rained out. It doesn't take forever. You don't need new equipment or special clothes and you don't need an expensive country club.

Baseball is no longer interesting. I recently heard Colin Cowherd report that more 18-34 year old American males watched Mixed Martial Arts on pay per view than watched the World Series. If that is a leading indicator, baseball is in deep shit.

Theisman Rhymes with Heisman

When I was in graduate school, we had a fellow student with the last name of Thiesman. She was Joe's cousin. She pronounced the name "Theeeesman, not Theisman." The folks at Notre Dame know how to market sports, don't they?

Athletes and Crime

Athletes have an image problem. They just plain commit too many indiscretions. Sometimes these indiscretions are crimes, like rapes and dog fighting—even killing dogs. Michael Vick recently publically complained that he is being treated unfairly by referees. My friend, Metz thinks this is because most refs are dog owners. I guess the lesson here is, if you play professional football and you are good at playing football, you can recover. Another lesson is that is more difficult to recover your values as an endorser of products than as a player. We maybe should call this the Tiger factor.

12

Boomers and People Boomers Should Respect

Hero (*Webster*: Exhibiting great courage or valor). It strikes me that we have depreciated the word hero. To me it has always meant someone who did something exceptionally valorous and out of the ordinary that you would not expect a normal person to do. That they reached outside of themselves.

As a kid, many of us knew that Audie Murphy was a hero. And he was. He tried to enlist in WWII from the get go, but he was a very runty 15 year old and was turned down. The next year, still runty at 16, his sister altered his birth certificate and he enlisted. He won 33 wartime medals, including the Congressional Medal of Honor. After WWII ended he wrote *To Hell and Back* about his war experiences. He then starred in the movie version of the book.

When we played war we all wanted to be Audie Murphy. Interestingly many of us still remember him. His grave in Arlington National Cemetery is the 2nd most visited grave, after JFK's, of course. For early Boomers he was the definition of a hero, the gold standard. But the term now is used all the time. Like money depreciates in value as the supply is increased, it appears to me that the term hero depreciates as the hero supply increases. "The Today Show" is like the punch drug Fed, racing to increase the hero supply on a daily basis. When I mention this to my fellow Boomers, they sometimes get testy with me. I will try to explain what I mean when I mourn the depreciation of heroism.

Sully Sullenberger certainly acted with valor when his Airbus 320 went down in the Hudson River. He was well trained and he acted very coolly in a very danger filled situation, but I do not consider him to be a hero. He was a well trained, cool customer who did his job exceedingly well. I would like him to be my pilot anytime. I would like to have a martini with him. But a hero? A close friend of mine called me names when I told him that I did not consider Sully a hero. A hero for me is someone who puts their life in harm's way when they were not part of the deal and their life would not have been in danger if they had "minded their own beeswax," as we used to say. The guy, also in 2009, who jumped in front of the approaching subway in New York City to save the drunken woman who had fallen, is a hero to me. He could have been safe on the sidelines. Todd Beamer is a hero to me. Beamer lead the,"Are you guys ready, let's roll," aboard flight 92 headed for DC on 9/11. It is reported that "Let's Roll Guys" became a rallying cry for American Troops in Afghanistan. Todd and his "Guys" on that plane are all in my hero book.

But get this, in November 2009 on the NBC "Today Show," Meredith was interviewing a train operator that avoided an accident. The modest woman claimed, "she was just doing her job." Meredith responded with "thank goodness she knows how to do her job; that is a hero." I think that may be the new NBC working definition of hero. Sully and the nameless train operator were doing their jobs very well; in my book Todd and his guys are heroes. It is gratifying that Sully did not consider himself a hero. He claimed he was only doing his job, his very risky job. He did not even look like a pilot. He didn't even look like an accountant. He looked like a third grade parochial school teacher.

People I would Like to Have a Martini With

I liked the movie *Bucket List* but I do not want to jump off a bridge tied to a bungee cord or travel to some exotic place that does not have air conditioning. I mostly don't want to go to third world, shit hole countries where even the streets smell like shit. So instead of a bucket list I am developing a list of people both living and dead with whom I would like to share a 5 p.m. martini with.

Dwight D. Eisenhower

President Eisenhower is the first President I remember. In a recently published recollection in *The Fort Worth Star Telegram* (January 24, 2011), I read that speaking in December 1949 to 3,500 people at the Will Rogers Coliseum in Fort Worth, he said, "Creeping paralysis of state paternalism can be as fatal as the destructive blow of an enemy... The fundamental principle of the dignity of the human soul written into the Constitution must be the guiding daily philosophy of every citizen lest we gradually lose the ability to think and act for ourselves." At the time he was President of Columbia University and testing the water for a presidential race. I wonder if they teach this at Columbia today. You know the answer.

John Updike

Updike died in January 2009. He was born in 1932, way too early to be a Baby Boomer, but Harry Angstrom, Rabbit, was in my reading a Boomer. I love the Rabbit novels. They amuse and in some ways frighten me; there was some of Harry in all early Boomers. At the same time exhilarated and frightened by the rapidly changing moirés.

Margaret Thatcher

She is greatest leader of our time. She has a big influence on the second greatest leader of our time. He is next.

Ronald Reagan

He is the second greatest leader, of our time. I read the other day that President Reagan would never take his suit coat off in the oval office. This was out of respect for his predecessors. I am sure one was Eisenhower. A liberal journalist suggested that this was because he was "acting." I really don't care. If he was acting, he still is my greatest President of our time.

Art Laffer

He really gets it. He was recently an answer on Jeopardy. He once told Ronald Reagan that the person most responsible for electing him President was Jimmy Carter. Reagan reportedly laughed.

Ringo Star

"Everything government touches turns to crap." Enough said and it proves that all that dope did not cloud his perceptions.

Keith Richards

I just saw him on *CBS Sunday Morning.* WOW!

Chief Justice John Roberts

He understands the importance of the private sector in the economy. This is a scarce commodity in most lawyers from pointy headed US law schools and even scarcer on the Supremes.

Jack Nicklaus

The non Tiger!

Vince Lombardi

Hey, I grew up in Wisconsin!

TV Cooks

Who would have predicted that cooking would be a big draw on TV? When we were kids our mothers warmed up Mrs. Filbert's Fish Sticks in the oven before they went out for drinks and dinner. No, let me take that back. My mother taught me how to turn on the oven so I could warm up Mrs. Filbert's Fish sticks for my twin sister and me. Now people build fancy kitchens and watch cooking channels, not shows, channels.

I guess all these celebrity chefs owe thanks to Julia Child. In fact, we all owe her. I just learned from a friendly reviewer that she was a spy for us in China during WWII.

I have heard many TV chefs praise Emeril for their current popularity. Most men like Giada, she clearly has the nicest tits and when she cooks she bends forward—a lot. I think you can learn a lot from Mario and Anne Burrell, and the Barefoot Contessa. Alton Brown reminds me of my high school science teachers, with the important exception that he teaches some very useful information.

Henry Kissinger (No reason needed)

Karl Rove (Also no reason needed)

Rudy Giuliani

"I think the Republican Party would be well advised to get the heck out of people's bedrooms." Enough said,

Shelby Steele

If you don't know Shelby Steel, read "Obama and the Burden of Exceptionalism," *The Wall Street Journal*, October 1, 2011, p.A17. You will want to know him!

Finally, William Faulkner

Faulkner moved to the University of Virginia to be its first writer in residence and then retired to the country. It was local legend that he walked on "The Lawn" and that during the Kennedy Administration he was invited to have dinner at the White House. He responded that it was too far to go to dinner with "people" you had never met.

13

The End: Not Death, The End of My Scouting Report

Good Parenting

Let me add a few extraneous thoughts for you to consider. You're running out of time to have much influence on your kids and grandchildren, but give some thought to some "wisdoms" you can pass on, if they will listen. You have to be careful here as they may act as if they are listening, but always keep in mind they may be jockeying for position in your will or for that matter, texting.

Tell your kids and their kids, anyone who will listen, not to go hiking in dangerous places. I am not talking about Yellowstone. I am not even talking about downtown Minneapolis at night. I am talking about places like North Korea or Iran. They might get arrested. If you were lost or claim to be lost, it will not likely matter. They will simply say you entered without permission. And they might charge you with working for the CIA. I find that argument quite persuasive. I don't find the lost argument anywhere near as plausible as the CIA argument. I believe people to be rational and there is no rational reason to be in these places unless you are getting paid (a lot), or are profoundly stupid. To add insult to injury, we, I guess I mean taxpayers, are asked to pony up tax revenue to get these "adventuresome" kids out of harm's way. Sometimes these "kids" work for former Vice Presidents, Nobel Prize Winners, and Academy Award winners, sometimes all rolled up into one person, none other than Al Gore. Do you think he paid to get them out? There was some comic relief; President Clinton even upstaged Gore on his glorious moment of negotiating their release. Bill showed up first! His timing has always been superb.

But you have to admit there are kids out there doing a lot of risky things. Really stupid things like car surfing or sailing around the world on summer vacation between first and second grade. This is really not new. We car surfed in the early 1960s and yes, beer was involved. But no one seemed to care. And no one got hurt. It actually helped that we were drinking, as we were "looser" if we fell off. Importantly, we didn't get lost and never required "bribes" for a release.

Today, something goes cattywampus, and governments spend a lot of money trying to put things right. This really pisses me off because I don't think the government has any business fixing up shitty parenting. Now if you leave your kid locked in a car on a 105 degree day in Phoenix you could well go to jail. But, if you send her around the world in a sailboat, you get to, exclusively, meet Matt on "The Today Show," I hate asymmetrical things. But I also don't think government can solve these problems. In fact, government adds to the problem by rescuing the bad decision makers. Moral hazard again.

So, I propose an organization called, "Mothers Yelling Against Stupid Schemes." This could well solve the problem. When some publicity seeking father encourages his daughter to hike to Korea or to sail twice around the world alone, the acronym, MYASS steps in. As in, My Ass you're sailing around the world, MYASS puts an end to it. I think mothers are much more sensible about such things than fathers. Best of all, this need not be a governmental program. Even better, MYASS can put pressure on the news to not publicize risky kid behavior. That would greatly decrease the incentive to do it in the first place. Maybe MADD would volunteer some help in getting this going. They have already figured out how to organize pissed off mothers and could give very good advice on how to proceed. They also can teach them how to raise money.

Retirement

A thought on retirement, Don't. From what I have observed, retirement is deadly. As you age your golf game does not improve. You look like an old fool out there.

The best statement I have ever heard about not retiring was made by Bea Arthur, of Maude fame and many other stage roles. I saw an interview with her on "CBS Sunday Morning." It was a 30 year retrospective that played on Labor Day 2009. Ms. Arthur who had died earlier in 2009 was asked on the clip why she didn't retire. Her reply was that it was easy to do what you love to do. She followed up by saying that people who care about their jobs don't like to retire. "It's glorious," she said. The lesson I took from this is not to retire, but quit your job now if you don't like it and find something you can do happily until you're 95, no dead.

If you don't take this advice and you do retire, limit yourself to one month each of solitaire or hearts on your computer. Refrain from sending email jokes to your friends. Okay—one joke a week. Once you are retired you have no need to send emails to distribution lists. If you have the idea to send an email to a distribution list think about it for a week. This also holds for jokes—perhaps more importantly for jokes. In fact, remove the "reply to all" function from your computer. Remember you are retired, hardly anyone cares about what you think, and if it is about a meeting, you're not invited.

If you wear bifocals or for that matter only "cheaters" be careful when you walk down steps carrying a case of wine. It is wise to take them off. When you trip it could be a big loss. In fact, you might start looking around for a one floor house.

Cultivate the few family and friends you have left. My father and my father in law were completely different personalities from completely different backgrounds. They had only one piece of advice in common. That one piece of wisdom was how few friends we would have as we aged. "You would be lucky if you can count them on one hand." Some would of course die, but mostly they come and go. Often it happens when a new woman enters the scene. It also is the case that we all move about so much these days.

Perhaps, most importantly, avoid high maintenance people. You will always be surprised by their behavior, and they never reciprocate. Life is a reciprocating business. Friends are there for you, even when you don't need them. More importantly, they are there when you do need them. As we all have learned, I hope, is that from such little things as keeping in touch to such big things as being there when needed, friends are precious. I am not advocating that you be there to insure that you have friends, but rather that you be there because they are your friend. If you do you will have friends. I am also saying that you should be in touch. How else would you know if you should be there? Return to the beginning of this story, Patricia was there for Susan and me in 2008 for the big C. I met her in August 1967 my first day at UVA. Susan met her in December 1968. In 2008, forty one years later, she was learning how to change my urine bag and giving moral support to Susan.

Get a dog, even if you have never had one. Dogs are loving and loyal. When you return home, your dog is always happy to see you. Importantly, they get you out of the house for walks. You will meet many people when you are walking your dog. And remember the friend who told me she defined heaven as where all your past dogs come running to greet you. It would be sad to arrive ungreeted. Horses count here too, but mostly for women. I am not sure about cats. I have a hard time understanding cat love. Maybe that's because they make my eyes water.

Be careful what you wear. T-shirts are okay, but T-shirts that say things like, "Where in the Hell is Ideal Corners," on them are not okay. Get some T-shirts from your Alma Mater, if you went to a decent place. Otherwise buy some from a good place and people will assume you went there. Try a place with a good football team. If not, buy some plain T-shirts with nice material, the kind with thicker fabric. Never wear T-shirts you can read a newspaper through. You might also think twice about wearing your cell phone on a cord around your neck so you don't lose it.

You will be tempted in the spring to get out your Topsiders and wear them. After all they are part of your Baby Boomer Psyche. But it is still a bit chilly so you will reach for some white socks. Stop. Never, ever wear topsiders with socks. It is the only binding fashion rule of Baby Boomers. Don't embarrass yourself, maintain some dignity. On second thought, you're 60, wear whatever you want. Screw the fashion rules.

Finally

Be interesting. Learn something new. If you find yourself up to your ass in shit, say shit. Move about. If you don't know how to play gin rummy, learn how. Your golf game will decline and you can always go to the golf club and play gin rummy in the locker room with the other old farts. My old friend Charlie started to play golf with his wife and he reported that saying, "Nice shot, honey," 125 times in nine holes, isn't all that bad.

Neil Cavuto is one of my favorites on TV. The other day I heard him say at the end of his show on Fox, "My Irish mother told me that life is a snap shot, pray you don't look worse in the next one." Think of the physical self abuse Ringo Starr put his body through. He turned 70 in July 2010. Buck up Bucko, you can make it too. Ringo actually looked pretty good in the picture in the paper. We still love him and he is way older than 64.

Thornton Wilder wrote in *Our Town*, "You're twenty-one, you make a decision and the next minute you're sixty-four." The first of us Boomers have six years to catch up on what we wanted to do and didn't before we were 70. Get after it.

If you like martinis, try some Brokers Gin. It is really good and also is cheaper than the other call brands. It's distilled the traditional way, using a copper pot still. And it comes from London. If you don't like martinis, learn to like them. If you once liked to smoke buy a pack. They go well with a martini and at your age they are not going to kill you and, most importantly, if you have one first thing in the morning it will keep you "regular." If you need more than that in retirement, I can't help you.

Keep doing whatever it is you do even though "it gets harder as you get older—and farther away as you get closer." Stephen Stills must like puns.

ILLUSTRATION SOURCES

All four cartoons were drawn specifically for this book by the author's long time friend Mark Seidl.

Illustrations in order:

Toboggan chute photo was taken by the author's maternal grandfather around 1955. It was taken on a "new-fangled" 3D camera.

The Fraternity House Scouting Party photo was made for the author for a fraternity newsletter in 1966 when he was the fraternity president.

The Jack Pine Savage lawn decoration and local village pollution pictures were taken by the author.

The Ripon College cast picture from *Come Back Little Sheba* was taken by a Ripon College photographer in 1963 and was a gift from the director, Professor Philip Clarkson.

The picture of Susan and Ryan with President Clinton in The White House was a gift from a University of Texas at Arlington photographer. It was taken when the author was a guest of President Clinton at the White House. The occasion was to recognize the UTA Wheel Chair BB team winning the Wheel Chair BB national championship, 1992.

The picture of Susan and Ryan Amacher with Jesse Jackson was a gift from a *Greenville News* photographer as all three emerged from an airplane at the Greenville/Spartanburg Airport. Jackson was on his way to Clemson for a speech. Jackson had spent the flight discussing race issues and Clemson University with Ryan and Susan, around 1988.

Author picture was taken by Shawn Smith, Thomas Reprographics.

CPSIA information can be obtained at www.ICGtesting.com
Printed in the USA
BVOW072318011112

304501BV00002B/18/P